Pathways
TO
Greatness

Seventy-seven inspirational essays from
The Greatness Project

by Scott Asalone and Jan Sparrow

Great Insights Press
Trenton, NJ
www.GreatInsightsPress.com

Great Insights Press, Inc.
101 Renfrew Avenue
Trenton, NJ 08618
www.GreatInsightsPress.com

ISBN 978-0-9673212-4-0

Cover and text design by
ThreeBears.com
Princeton, NJ

CONTENTS

Acknowledgments

So many people were involved in our study of greatness and the writing of this book. Specifically we would like to thank Robert Calabrese for his support and encouragement, Meredith Gould for her thoughtful insights and editing, Katie Losch for finding all the little things we missed, Paul Schindel and the staff at Three Bears for their great work on the look and feel of our book, Anthony Asalone from Great Insights Press for his help in publishing our book, and to all of our faithful readers who shared ideas, stories, and their journeys to greatness with us. Thank you. May all of you continue to live your greatness.

Introduction

Albany, New York. Year: 2000. We were working with a financial services organization that wanted to enhance its teamwork. After an early morning presentation that received a lukewarm reception, we met with established work teams. At each meeting we offered our most positive and realistic best practices for team productivity. And at each meeting we were told, "You can't do that in Albany."

Although our recommendations were grounded in research and based on the proven success of hundreds of similar teams, client resistance continued. Try as we might to encourage, cajole, influence, and even beg these teams to at least try something new, they insisted, "You can't do that in Albany, but…"

Finally, our day almost over, we met with the last team on the schedule. Discouraged from the defensive nature of earlier encounters, we began our session with this caveat, "We know you can't do most of this in Albany…"

The team leader challenged us almost immediately. "What do you mean we can't implement these ideas in Albany? We believe it's a great environment. There are tremendous possibilities here and we're up 25 percent this year and believe we can do more. What ideas do *you* have to offer?" Stunned, we completed our final meeting and left, shaking our heads.

Why is it that everything being equal, some people and organizations will rise to the top while others will languish? Are there characteristics, personalities, or organizational dimensions that will allow people or organizations to flourish even during difficult times? Thus was born THE GREATNESS PROJECT™.

We launched THE GREATNESS PROJECT with an email survey to

friends and associates, asking broad questions about greatness and their personal views on the subject. (see Appendix A for the original survey.) Their responses were amazing. Not only were our respondents very forthcoming about their beliefs about greatness, but they offered wonderful stories to illustrate their beliefs. They also forwarded our survey to friends and associates. But what propelled us even more powerfully forward into this work was their request to know more about our findings. They, too, wanted to identify characteristics of great individuals and to understand more about whether these features are learned or genetic.

Our study of greatness was also driven by our respondents' desire to explore realms of human capacity currently being ignored. Within our celebrity-driven culture, money and possessions have become key indicators of greatness. We were exhorted to push past mere social status to examine values, beliefs, and aspirations; to explore the extent and power of human spirit and drive. Nowhere, in all the survey data we received, the dialogues we held, or at conferences we led, did anyone ever equate human greatness with achieving status or acquiring wealth.

It's a truism that once you begin looking for something you tend to see it more often. That's what soon happened for us. In our day-to-day lives we began noticing individuals who embodied the characteristics we were researching. Some, like Mother Theresa of Calcutta, or Rudy Guiliani were also identified by respondents as examples of greatness. Others, like Sammy, who pumped gas near our office, we noticed because of their enthusiasm for work and life. He was so energized and energizing that cars lined up at his station no matter what the cost of gasoline. We saw, in Sammy and others like him, a greatness of spirit.

What especially enhanced our study were the conferences and workshops we've been privileged to facilitate over the years. Our conversations with individuals about their own struggle to unleash greatness provided powerful incentive for us to continue THE GREATNESS PROJECT. Admittedly, our research is not scientific but a compilation of survey data, anecdotes, musings, and synopses of significant discoveries in diverse fields. What we hope to offer are specific behavioral-based concepts that anyone can employ to achieve personal greatness.

These articles have been placed in chronological order so you may see the development of thought from our survey respondents and other sources. Whenever we've made reference to other works, we've provided bibliographic information so you may track down the original research, article, or book if you so desire.

We hope you are inspired, enlightened, and amused by what you read here. More importantly, we hope that as you read, you will see yourself reflected and thereby understand the most important premise of this work; there is greatness within all of us.

Enjoy.

Scott Asalone   Jan Sparrow

Who Is in Control?

August 2001

When you awake each morning, even before you get out of bed, try asking yourself this question, "Who is in charge of my life?"

Most of us would laugh and claim that we were, of course, in charge. Interestingly enough, our comments, complaints, and nonverbal reactions during the day might reveal quite the opposite belief. Many of us blame and complain about "those people" who control our life. Our research indicates that individuals who believe they are striving for or achieving greatness have a sense of power over their destiny.

Power over destiny is not just about choosing a job, partner, or home, it's about choosing our quality of life and the energy (or power) surrounding it. Respondents who wrote to us about choices they've made or decisions they were anticipating, revealed that the decisions were theirs to be made freely. They reveled in this power of choice, knowing that they were creating their own legacy.

We've discovered another piece of research that dovetails nicely with our own. Using a database of more than 1500 people from more than 40 different organizations in North America, Essi Systems discovered information about stress in the workplace:

> "Our extensive testing revealed that a single factor had a greater impact than any other on the individual employee's ability to manage work pressures, stay healthy and maintain an optimal state of productivity during times of change. We call this key factor personal power and we define it as knowing that you have the inner capacity to give and receive

11

what you want and need to do your job well. In other words, **personal power** is a sense of inner security that you can meet whatever challenges you may face. **It means acting with confidence because you have control over your time, resources, important information, work load, etc.**"
(Emphasis ours)

Having control over our life does not mean that we have all elements aligned so that nothing goes wrong. On the contrary, it means that when things do go wrong, we don't look for someone else to blame or someone else to fix it. Instead, we ask, "What can I do about this?" This is the personal power that individuals who seek greatness affirm constantly and consistently. Great individuals are in control of their lives and, ultimately, their destiny.

Greatness In Adversity

September 2001

September 11, 2001 will live forever in our memory. Humans rise to greatness in times of adversity. We unfold the best of who we are and share it with the world. Stories of heroism are just beginning to emerge from the rubble of the World Trade Center.

Our experience of the tragedy was minor by comparison but caused us to reflect. We passed through the World Trade Center heading to midtown Manhattan approximately 45 minutes before the first plane hit. We joined the masses on the streets of New York, stunned by what had happened.

Not able to leave the city, we walked down to 33rd Street. At lunch, we found ourselves sitting next to two men who had been on the 61st floor of the South Tower of the World Trade Center when the airplane hit. They were still in shock. And then it happened: *hearing how we were stranded in the city overnight, they said they had a large hotel room and that we could share it.*

Later, we walked toward Penn Station and arrived just as one last train was allowed to leave for New Jersey. It quickly filled to capacity and we were still on the platform. And then it happened: *seeing the group, the engineer opened up his compartment and squeezed in all ten of us.* "I just couldn't leave you there," he said.

Getting off the train in Newark, we tried getting to our car in Jersey City. After 45 minutes, the taxi cab returned to the station because the roads were gridlocked. And then it happened again: *the cab driver refused to charge us because he had not gotten us to our destination.*

Ultimately, an empty train was brought to Newark to shuttle

passengers south. After boarding, we asked about tickets and were told that NJ Transit was not charging anyone to ride. These were all acts of greatness.

Our ongoing experience was that even people at a distance from the day's terror reached out to others. Why does our greatness rise noticeably to the surface during adversity? Perhaps, it's because at that moment the focus is not on us, but on helping others around us. Everywhere we turned, whether in New York or in New Jersey, people wanted to do anything they could to help; to be a part of the effort to bring about greater peace and stability.

In our research, we've found that for many of us greatness is measured by what we can do for those around us. Whether it's the simple act of offering shelter, transportation to safety, or a free ride, placing self-interest aside for the good of others brings out the best in us.

Now is a time for greatness; for us, for our nation.

Characteristics of Great Leaders During Adversity
September 2001

After the terrorist attack on September 11, 2001, we called around the country to find out if there was anything we could do for leaders we know. We heard them ask these questions: "What now? How do we begin to move forward from this?" Leadership is even more essential now. We need a model to examine.

One role model who is being recognized internationally for his leadership at this time of crisis is New York City's mayor, Rudolph Giuliani. Watching Giuliani, we noticed characteristics emerge that are consistent with what THE GREATNESS PROJECT and what recent Harvard research reveals about great leaders. We present these characteristics now, hoping that they'll help to enhance your leadership during this challenging time.

IN CONTROL

Minutes, hours, and days after the attack, Giuliani took swift control of what he could. He closed the bridges and tunnels and coordinated relief efforts. He did not run into the buildings nor fret about what could've been done. Being "in control" means having an awareness of what can be controlled and then letting the rest go. Giuliani did the best job he possibly could and allowed others to do theirs.

ABILITY TO LIVE WITH PARADOX

Great leaders are able to live with paradox. They are able to be totally **realistic** about what they face and how bad it is while

15

simultaneously being **optimistic** about the future.

While speaking to the public, Giuliani never held back how bad the devastation was, but also spoke of the future of New York. He was able to live with the paradox.

RESOLUTE

Being resolute means that you create, for yourself and others, rituals that allow you to keep going in the face of tragedy. Short-term gains need to be accomplished until people can feel clear to focus on long-term goals.

Giuliani's immediate focus was on the steps necessary to rescue as many people as possible. When that goal was achieved as much as was humanly possible, he turned everyone's attention toward recovery. He helped others accomplish daily tasks to get them past immediate and short-term inertia.

PASSIONATE

At the Yankee Stadium service, Giuliani broke down and cried. It was authentic, natural, and revealed his values to all. Showing emotion at times of difficulty allows others to realize how we're all in this together.

STEADY

During times of difficulty, leaders are expected to be steady. In the hours and days after the attack, it was reported that Giuliani "seemed to be everywhere." He was present to those who needed him; being their strength, crying with them, and helping them to focus on what needed to be done. This steadiness is not possible without an underlying belief system that's stronger than the waves of change crashing over us.

ABIDING FAITH IN HUMAN NATURE

Whenever Giuliani met with reporters, he lauded the police, fire fighters, rescue workers, and volunteers. It was always about them, not about him. In lifting up others as examples, great leaders make it possible for everyone to believe that they, too, can be heroic.

What Do You Believe?
October 2001

Why does tragedy make us examine our lives more closely? Since September 11, many of us have taken time to contemplate what's important, and why we do what we do. Some fascinating statistics are emerging about how people's behavior has changed since the terrorist attack.

For example, attendance at religious services increased 120% in the days immediately following the attack. At the same time, the sale of expensive shoes doubled and car sales climbed. When contemplating their life, individuals clearly react differently and stress different values.

According to our research, a durable belief in deeper values is a characteristic of greatness. Our respondents constantly refer to their fundamental belief in something larger than the self. For 100% of our participants, greatness is seen as something above and beyond a job, title, possessions, or wealth. Greatness is expressed in values such as love of family, integrity, honesty, helping others, or awareness of a divine presence.

Belief in a divine being or a universal value is more than just an idea for those who seek greatness, it's what drives them. More than money or status, great individuals are those who strive for higher ideals and goals because they believe there's a purpose for doing so and it's the purpose for their life.

One respondent phrased it this way:

"Personal greatness occurs when I feel my priorities in life are in balance and that I am being what I believe God is calling me to be in work, in relationships, in my family, with my family, with my community, etc. This is tough to achieve, since I believe I'm called to do more than acquire wealth, belongings and corporate stature, since they will not count for much in the end."

The events of September 11 prompted many people to re-evaluate their lives, asking these big questions: "What is important to me?" "What matters?" "Why do I do what I do?"

You might ask yourself these questions and then notice how your answers compare to the reality of your life. Are your beliefs focusing and driving your life?

The Gift of Gratitude
November 2001

Gratitude doesn't happen only at the Thanksgiving dinner table, it's a core value of those striving for greatness, one that propels them to give to others.

We notice a pattern in responses to our initial survey on greatness. Our respondents are grateful for what they have, who they are, or what they have accomplished. Some mention feeling "lucky" while others use the word "blessed." Some do not use those actual words but write that they are aware of the many benefits they have. This concurs with a recent *Harvard Business Review* article about some top performers in business. All admitted feeling "lucky" about where they were, who they were, and how they've succeeded.

Great individuals move through life with the strong belief that they've been given gifts and abilities. This is not self-promotion or self-aggrandizement, but an authentic feeling that they have something to share. Of course, they're also aware that they've learned and developed their special skills, but that does not reduce their feelings of gratitude.

This contrasts with a prevailing belief that it's arrogant or conceited to believe in your own greatness. We say that a true "attitude of gratitude" provides balance. When gratitude is present, a person will not be demanding, threatening, or demean anyone else because they believe that whatever they personally have is a gift. Gifts are meant to be shared. Gratitude changes our perspective on life.

In our greatness study we've found that this feeling of gratitude is not a stagnant awareness; it's a catalyst for movement. Fifty percent of our respondents mentioned or alluded to feeling grateful and thus being inspired or driven to help others. One respondent put it this way:

> *"I think that personal greatness is passing on to others what I have received. I have received many wonderful gifts.... My greatness has to do with seizing opportunities to pass these values and charisms on to other people and especially to generations that follow."*

Asking "What am I grateful for?" helps place life in perspective. The answer helps us discover what really matters to us. And why are we driven to give our very best? For many of our survey respondents, it's because they know they have much to give. They are grateful and so they want to give back.

Resolutions That Are Catalysts for Revolutions
December 2001

As we began creating this year's final issue of THE GREATNESS PROJECT, we had planned to focus on resolutions individuals make or the changes those resolutions create. But then we picked up the January issue of *Fast Company* which had an interview with Peter Koestenbaum, author of *Leadership: The Inner Side of Greatness.* One of today's experts in leadership, Koestenbaum's comments reflect much of what we wanted to write, so we're going to share his wisdom with you.

As we approach the New Year, we all make resolutions. The choice to be or do something differently is extremely important and can radically affect our lives. Koestenbaum adds, "Unless the distant goals of meaning, greatness, and destiny are addressed, we can't make an intelligent decision about what to do tomorrow morning. Nothing is more practical than for people to deepen themselves."

Reflecting on the tragedy of September 11, Koestenbaum observes that:

> *"To be a leader is to be awake and alert, to be dissatisfied at all times. After the wake-up call (of September 11) you can never allow life to be anything less than great. We must resolve to work (and live) with greatness and never forget to do so again. Every day is a concert, a Nobel-prize ceremony, or an Olympic victory. More than ever, we should celebrate the artists in business, the reformers in life, and the missionaries in organizations. It's your highest responsibility: protect your sense of destiny, greatness, dignity, and hope."*

How can you become more resolute about greatness in 2002? He suggests, "Ask yourself the big questions: What have I done wrong in my life? What must I do right?"

We say it's worth taking the time to redefine yourself and how you work. Write down your new work-life description. Revise it. And make that revision an oath, a conversion. What you are promising is to become the person that you were meant to be. That's your greatest responsibility right now. It's the ultimate New Year's resolution.

Great individuals realize that they cannot force change upon those around them, but can only change themselves. Even without attempting to change others, the New Year's resolutions that will help you become your very best self, may also revolutionize the lives of those around you.

Are You Still Resolved?
January 2002

Less than a month has passed since we created resolutions to take us through this year. What has happened? If surveys are correct, most of us abandon New Year's resolutions after the third week. Not so for those who are seen as great. Individuals who achieve greatness do not miraculously achieve it in one great act. They identify ways of living that they commit to and reinforce on a daily basis. Aristotle put it well, *"We are what we repeatedly do. Excellence, then, is not an act, but a habit."*

So, then, who are you? Are you a blend of mediocre and half-hearted attempts? Are you a composite of a constant striving for goals you've set? It's not "practice that makes perfect," but "**perfect** practice that makes perfect."

Perfect practice is attempting to do your very best all the time so that if there's one single moment when your best is required, you are already practiced at it. Our survey revealed that individuals committed to achieving greatness do not wait for a single moment to make them great. They know greatness will be achieved by daily striving, learning, and growing toward their best. One respondent put it this way:

> *"I don't think I have reached personal greatness at this point in my life because I know there are so many things I could improve upon in terms of knowledge, managing, leading, having the vision, being a mother, or daughter, etc., but given that, I do my very best on a **daily basis**… Ultimately, I try my very best to be attentive to the task at hand, to make personal*

*contact with people I work with **on a daily basis** and service the client, whoever that might be for the task at hand."* (emphasis ours)

Many of us are challenged by our longing to see progress, some sort of indication that lets us know we're getting somewhere. It's easy to chart progress in business or a stock portfolio. Keeping tabs on your own growth is more challenging. Rededicating yourself to your quest each and every day could be the only progress you know.

So, now that we're in the third week of the year, what are you resolving to do on a daily basis? How are you resolving to live? These are the habits that will create a legacy, so choose wisely and commit daily.

Unleash the Magic
February 2002

Just before Todd Eldridge took the ice for the men's individual program, Olympic commentator Scott Hamilton made this suggestion: "He needs to relax and just skate." Less than a minute into his long program, Todd fell, prompting Scott to comment that skaters can't think about their program, they just have to skate it. After the fall, Todd grew more confident the longer he skated. He had relaxed.

Great athletes, musicians, actors, and business people remark about moments when the world seems to recede and they're alone in their element. Everything comes together flawlessly; it almost seems like magic. These moments of personal greatness that we long to repeat often elude us because we can't force them. One survey respondent wrote, "These mystical moments are not something that can be expected or promoted in any way. They have always come into my consciousness with a note of surprise and mystery." How can we generate more of these moments without forcing them?

PREPARATION

Whatever our goal, we have to prepare so that we know our craft extremely well; it becomes part of us. In his autobiography, Jack Welch, former CEO of GE, describes his own intense research before meeting with division heads. During the meeting, he'd open up a discussion about possibilities and even he would be amazed by the creative dialogue that emerged.

Our preparation, which can take many forms, readies us for our next great moment. "I am in that process right now, preparing with intense reading, reflection, writing, prayer, and experimenting with a new way of offering myself to the world around me," wrote one of our respondents. Whatever our goal, preparation makes us ready for magic moments.

LETTING GO

Once in the flow of a great moment, we often don't know how it happened. Sure we tried our best, but still end up wondering, "Why this time…why now?" If we're honest with ourselves, we'll recognize that we probably just relaxed and let it happen. In the world of sports this is called "muscle memory" and describes that moment when the body simply responds because of training. For us, perhaps "greatness memory" becomes possible when we practice our discipline enough so that it becomes part of us and we can allow greatness memory to take over.

Ultimately, we can open ourselves to more and more moments when everything flows:

> *"I know when I'm in moments of personal greatness. I feel very light and buoyant as if my words are flowing without effort and my thoughts are very clear. I'm doing what I was meant to be doing and in doing so the work, the art, and the words that come forth are absolutely beautiful and in no need of alteration."*
> (Survey respondent)

Preparation and then letting go may seem like a simple technique, but for most of us it means relinquishing control. Ideally, control is mastered in practice; magic is unleashed in the moment.

Are We Fully Alive?
March 2002

Are you fully alive? It seems obvious that you're alive because you're reading this article! But if your friends, family and colleagues describe you, would they say that you are "fully alive?"

Being fully alive does not mean just eating, sleeping and breathing, it means that we exude energy. We're alive with life and everyone who comes in contact with us is aware of our exhilaration. How does this translate into greatness?

Examine the current literature on excellence in the corporate, spiritual, and everyday world. People who encounter great individuals describe them in words like "energetic," "lively," and "passionate." Great individuals live fully the hours they have on this planet and it's obvious to everyone around them.

Social scientists are examining how to help individuals become aware of life around them and how to live it fully. Their findings reveal that as people live life through the disciplines of awareness, focus, gratitude, inquisitiveness, and celebration they become alive to possibilities and fearless in the face of obstacles. They embolden themselves while simultaneously motivating everyone around them. Attaining this "aliveness" in the face of time pressure, peer pressure, and belief-system pressure is the challenge.

Time pressure conveys the idea that knowing answers rather than asking questions will help us save time. Peer pressure sometimes emerges in sideways glances and comments when we attempt to celebrate life more obviously. Belief-system pressure is perhaps, the greatest obstacle to being alive especially when interior beliefs dictate who we're supposed to be and how we're supposed to act. Far too often this is based on false notions about how a "professional" or an "adult" behaves.

How can we begin accessing the power of being fully alive? The greatest discipline is awareness. Most of us go through life half aware, hardly tasting the food we eat or listening to those around us. More data seems like overload because, believing more is better, we're already receiving too much information — hardly ever evaluating the quality of all the information we gather. Real knowledge that might make a difference is the wisdom gleaned through living fully with awareness.

Those who strive for greatness use their awareness of life to propel them to gratitude, inquisitiveness, and celebration. Energy flows out from them because energy is constantly flowing into them from many sources. They are fearless in their desire to experience all that life has to teach. Their fearlessness allows their energy to inspire all who come into contact with them.

Can you do this for yourself? Certainly you can, by developing the discipline of being fully aware of the world around you. A little more awareness each day will draw you into the spectacular reality of all that life provides and simultaneously transform you into someone who is fully alive.

Inquire Within!
April 2002

> *"Most of the significant advances in human history — great social and political reformations, artistic productions, unique inventions, etc. — have come not from rushing around but from being still. They required periods of deep and rigorous contemplation, for only in this way can we escape the clamor of outer voices that remind us of "how we've always done it."*
>
> from *The Heart of a Leader*

Leadership, greatness, and self-help books are so prolific that upon entering any bookstore you can't help but notice the latest multi-step approach to achieving something. Yet, an inner voice rebels against this simplicity: "If it's this easy, why isn't everyone attaining greatness?" If all we have to do is study the latest quick fix and apply its ideas, changing the world should be simple, right? Wrong.

Reality is much more complex. Achieving substantial change in our lives requires first "owning" our beliefs and goals. Next, we have to change ourselves and that's no easy task. Reading books about steps that helped others is only a start. Internalizing what we've read, discerning and then taking our own steps toward being authentic is tougher.

There's no substitute for making room for interior time, that quiet time dedicated to developing values, beliefs, and priorities. Almost all our survey respondents who expressed their personal beliefs and values, also commented about how much they enjoyed considering questions they had not thought about in a while — or at all.

Staking time out for personal introspection is not superfluous, it's essential. Whether you secure time while commuting to work or by taking time away for solitude, the journey to being our best self requires asking key questions and contemplating the answers alone. Some of these fundamental questions are: Who am I? Who do I want to be? What do I believe? What are my values? What is my purpose in life? How does this affect those around me? Answering these essential questions will help you develop authentic inner strength and imagination.

No book can provide the level of insight that dedicated introspection provides. It's through generative "alone time" that beliefs become guidelines and dreams become reality.

The Difference Is Zeal!
May 2002

In a recent interview, Jack Welch, former CEO of GE, was asked, "What separates the best people in an organization from the rest?" The answer, he said, was simple. The best people share one primary characteristic: passion.

We do not easily challenge such a leadership guru, but perhaps current overuse of the word "passion" obscures what he really meant. Passion is often used to characterize an almost palpable energy and drive; that's entirely correct. However, properly defined, passion also refers to a powerful emotion focused primarily on desire or love. That's not what most of us have in mind when we talk about passionate individuals or having passion for what we do.

Only 2% of THE GREATNESS PROJECT respondents used the word "passion" or "passionate" to identify greatness. And yet, while describing great individuals or specific attributes, they noted how these individuals always have an intense drive for what they do, and that is evident in their work, their attitude, their communication, and their lives. Their definitions of greatness included action words such as "persistence," "continually improve," and "movement" directed toward ideals and goals such as "personal integrity," "balance," and "a sense of accomplishment."

We say that the attribute they've repeatedly described is actually "zeal." Zeal is defined as "enthusiastic devotion to a cause, an ideal, or a goal and tireless diligence in its furtherance."

So what's the big deal about one word? The difference is that the definition not only properly describes what we see in great individuals, but it contains the steps necessary to attain zeal.

1. The first step involves identifying a goal, cause, or ideal. What do we really care about? What are we devoted to? Without an identifiable goal we become zombies, caught up in work and life without meaning. No one else can infuse our lives with meaning; that's our job.

2. The second step is not possible without the first. We can only become enthusiastic if there's something to become enthusiastic about. Clients constantly ask us to create enthusiasm in their organizations and employees. But, it's impossible to demand continuous enthusiasm if there are only tasks and no goal, cause, or ideal to attain.

In a recent interview, a leader said to us about his employees, "If they don't really love what they do, I would hope they'd go somewhere else and search until they find what they love." Once individuals discover a goal, cause, or ideal they love, enthusiasm comes easily.

3. The third step is the most difficult. It's easy to give up on goals; easy to say something can't be done. Great individuals enthusiastically embrace life and they do it with tireless diligence. Each day they have the choice between striving for success or giving up. The great ones don't give up.

One word, then, can be very powerful. Zeal identifies a characteristic we find in great individuals. They exude it, exclaim it, and live it. So, Jack, **zeal** is what separates great individuals from the rest.

Is Enough, Enough?
June 2002

When our phone rang two weeks ago, we assumed it was a typical request for our services, but this call in particular grabbed our interest. It was from a regional officer at a multi-national company who wanted us to provide client service training. We were intrigued because that region won a national quality service award four years in a row and was about to win again.

Why would they want training in an area of excellence? For us this raised an even broader question: what drives the greatest to want to become even better?

The individuals and groups we serve and study want to be something more than they are right now. It's not about awards or achievement for them. They seek something deeper and more intangible, something far beyond what would normally garner praise. This elusive characteristic is perhaps the one that really defines greatness although the desire to learn or do more is not, in fact, easily measured.

Although we've encountered this characteristic in our study and experience, we have not found it identified in the larger body of work on human greatness. Usually, the pursuit of excellence is defined in terms of achievement. We argue that achievement is just a byproduct of this characteristic that we are challenged to name. Words like restlessness, relentlessness, tenacity, and perfectionism do not seem to fully capture it.

In addition, this characteristic can be a double-edged sword. Individuals and groups driven by this characteristic also tend to suffer from never being quite satisfied. Being as focused as they are, they may find themselves not taking time to celebrate insights encountered along their journey to greatness. For some, this can lead to an imbalance: pursuit without concomitant and necessary rest periods. Care has to be taken so that energy can be renewed to continue the quest.

Our phone rang again that same week. This call was from a senior manager at another multi-national company. He had contacted his development director to request a coach. He was told he didn't need a coach; the organization was so impressed with his work they did not believe he needed any more development. When he called, he revealed his relentlessness when he said, "There's still so much I have to learn."

As long as we believe there's more to learn, more to do, or deeper levels of awareness to explore, we are driven by a characteristic that might be a key to unlock human greatness.

Can you feel it? Do you have it? What do you call it?

Because We Can
July 2002

The July 11 issue of *USA Today* had an article about the "mega-mansions" being built across the United States. Noting the average living space of families is increasing dramatically in America, the article highlighted families in Potomac, Maryland where an excessive number of these homes are being built.

When asked why a four-person family needed six bedrooms, nine bathrooms, a four-car garage, two home offices and multiple other rooms, the owner replied, "Because we can." We would add, paraphrasing the comedian George Carlin, that we need bigger places to store all of our stuff so we can go out and get more stuff.

Many individuals identify themselves exclusively by what they own, the position they have, or the money they earn. Their search for meaning becomes synonymous with getting more "stuff." It's precisely the search for meaning and how it's answered that differentiates those who seek greatness.

Our survey and readings lead us to posit that individuals who seek greatness do so as part of the search for meaning in life. They seek something greater than themselves and that will benefit others. In the process of discovery, they create meaning. They leave a legacy of striving, helping, caring, creating, or reaching that touches lives and encourages others to do the same.

At leadership conferences we always ask our two favorite questions. "How many of you woke up this morning and said, 'I think I'll be mediocre today?'" That usually gets a good laugh.

Then we ask, "How many of you woke up this morning and said, 'I will be great today.'" This is usually met with total silence. Why?

Because attempting to achieve greatness, attempting to find meaning in life, takes dedication and hard work.

THE GREATNESS PROJECT respondents who seek meaning in their lives are not waiting for answers to come from on high. They wake up each morning dedicated to producing that meaning in every action they take. Viktor Frankel in *Man's Search for Meaning* puts it much more eloquently (with apologies for non-inclusive language):

> *"Ultimately, man should not ask what the meaning of his life is, but rather he must recognize that it's he who is asked. In a word, each man is questioned by life; and he can only answer to life by answering for his own life; to life he can only respond by being responsible."*

We were challenged by one individual who asked, "It's so much work, why bother seeking greatness?" To answer this question we look at those who have sought greatness before us and those who still seek it. Ultimately, people seek greatness because striving to achieve it creates meaning in life, effects positive change, and leaves a legacy. We strive for greatness because we can.

What Matters?
August 2002

What really matters? That question arose based on responses received following our July edition of THE GREATNESS PROJECT, "Because We Can." In that article, we challenged the notion of gathering material possessions as proof of greatness and offered the idea that some individuals search for something else.

One respondent defined the drive behind the gathering of material possessions this way, "Getting stuff is a score-keeping mechanism, a visible score-keeping system." We can easily be caught up wanting to create presence through what, back in 1902, sociologist Thorstein Veblen termed, "conspicuous consumption." Society seduces us into believing that what we own defines us. Yet, as that respondent observed, "Bigger houses are not signs of the presence of greatness even though the owner might think so."

But there's another trap. If we do not believe greatness is found in material possessions or in wealth, we might believe we can find it in our job and get caught up in thinking that we are what we do.

A retired corporate executive offered this thought, "If our job prior to retirement defines us, then we're lost at retirement. Too many of our retired brethren also retire from that search [for greatness]. It takes on a different dimension or focus and is more related to what you can contribute based on what you learned."

It's a truism that we focus on what we value in life. Our choices about where and how to spend our precious time reveals what we value. Great individuals are those who focus on values that often differ from society, but are necessary for society to survive and thrive. Great individuals chart their own course according to what really matters to them.

We each have to evaluate our personal focus and time commitments to discover what matters most to us. Only after we identify the values we hold dear can we hear the clarion call of focusing our life on those values.

A homemaker in Northern Virginia, identified in her local paper as one of the "Loudoun's Greatest," shared this, "Greatness accomplished unconsciously is often the truest measure of greatness — doing good works for others with no consideration about personal sacrifice or recognition."

What matters to you?

The Power of Some Day
September 2002

Robert, an executive who works in the World Financial Center in New York, shared this powerful story with us. This past week, he was traveling from the World Financial Center across the Hudson River by ferry to Jersey City. He noticed someone he knew was in New York City on September 11, 2001 and struck up a conversation. They spoke about how things had changed in the past year.

As they walked to their respective cars in the parking lot, Robert noticed that the other person was getting into a new Thunderbird convertible with the license plate "mysomday." Questioning him about it, Robert received this reply. "My wife and I had always said that someday we would own a car like this. After September 11, we decided that there might not be a someday. So, we decided to fulfill one of our dreams."

Upon hearing this story we were struck by the power of "some day." It seems like a magical word in our society because it's the moment when many of us believe we will attain our fondest wishes, live out the life we have dreamed about, or act the way we really would like. We wait for when we'll be truly free to be, do, or have what we really want.

As we study great individuals, we see many examples of people who are not waiting for "some day" to pursue their dreams. They are not paralyzed by the power of rationalization. They are not allowing themselves to rest in the easy belief that they can't reach for their dreams right now because _____ (fill in the blank). Instead, they challenge themselves to move forward toward their dreams.

What steps are these individuals taking? First, they're asking what they want to have, do, or be. They allow themselves to dream. When was the last time you allowed yourself to dream and really believe you could live out your dreams? What if you dared to dream?

Once these individuals embrace their dreams, they take actions that either put them on track to attain their dreams, or they make radical choices that allow them to reach those dreams immediately. When one of our respondents realized what her real dream was, she gave up her Wall Street job and opted for teaching school at the edge of Chinatown. It's what she always wanted to do. Others are taking more gradual steps to reach their "some day."

We also noticed this about individuals who aggressively pursue their dreams: they encourage others to do the same. This is not about nagging. They are so excited about pursuing what they love that they can't help but encourage others to do the same.

What is your "some day"? Is there something you want to do, some different way you want to act, or something you want for you and your family? What holds you back? If anything is different since 9/11, it's that we're all more aware that "some day" is now. What are you waiting for?

What Do You See?

October 2002

You probably know the casual definition of the difference between an optimist and a pessimist. When a glass with liquid is placed in front of each, the pessimist will say it's half empty and the optimist will say it's half full.

Much research has gone into studying whether individuals who achieve great things are optimists or pessimists. The conclusion: pessimists are much more realistic. They can enumerate with extraordinary precision the amount of times they have succeeded and failed at a specific endeavor. Optimists, on the other hand, underestimate the number of times they've failed and overestimate the number of times they've succeeded. And while pessimists are much more realistic, optimists keep trying even in the face of over-whelming defeat; they'll often succeed — eventually (to the chagrin of pessimists).

But is it optimism, as commonly understood, that helps individuals cope with difficulties? As a prisoner of war in Vietnam, Admiral James Stockdale discovered that optimists would often not survive. They'd predict that they'd be free by a certain date, for example, Christmas. When Christmas came and went without being freed, they'd give up; some died.

What enables certain individuals to continue striving in the face of adversity, allowing them to not only survive but thrive? This characteristic has been identified as "strength," "endurance," "resilience," just to name a few.

In the September 2002 issue of *Harvard Business Review,* Warren Bennis identified it as "adaptive capacity, an almost magical ability to transcend adversity, and to emerge stronger than before."

We say that all these explanations are too vague about the presence and balance of optimism and pessimism. Pessimism, as defined in the *American Heritage College Dictionary*, is "a tendency to stress the negative or take the gloomiest possible view." Conversely, optimism is defined as "a tendency to expect the best possible outcome or dwell on the most hopeful aspects of a situation."

Optimists see pessimists as defeatists, whereas pessimists see optimists as starry-eyed. It seems like an either/or choice. Yet successful individuals we've interviewed and studied have a tremendous grasp on reality while simultaneously being able to create possibilities and believe in success. They seem to combine the best of optimism and pessimism. They are determined in the face of overwhelming odds, but not without a realistic awareness of their situation.

We have not identified the word to describe this middle ground between the common definitions of optimism and pessimism or specific behaviors attributed to it so we will continue to explore it in future research. (Reader input, as always, is welcome and encouraged.)

What we do know is that after great individuals acknowledge the level of liquid in the glass, they ask what they can do to fill it.

When you look at the glass, what do you see?

The Assumption of Positive Effect
November 2002

We recently created a second survey to provide more data on greatness. We began by providing a definition of greatness based on findings from our first survey. Greatness, according to our first group of respondents, is: "living out your personal value system every day."

People have taken us to task for such a loose definition. They legitimately claimed that any behavior could be justified as great if it aligned with a personal value system. Someone even challenged us by noting that the snipers in Virginia could have been acting out of their personal value system. We conceded but still noted that a review of our original data reveals that no one had placed a qualifier on greatness. No one defined greatness relative to ethics or stated that the results of greatness had to be community oriented.

What we found enlightening was that 95% of our respondents held a common notion when asked, "How do you know when you have achieved greatness?" Our respondents assumed that "living out your personal value system" would necessarily be measured by actions or words positively affecting others.

This assumption of positive effect is essential to understanding greatness and why anyone would want to achieve it. Seeking greatness in isolation from its effects is pure narcissism. Surely you've met individuals who are so busy making sure everyone knows who they are that they'll step on anyone to get into the spotlight. Intent on raising themselves above others, they focus on the characteristics of leadership, greatness, etc., but only for self-gratification.

The assumption of positive effect provides a base line, so that greatness is always judged by a positive return. If an individual is said to be great, we assume that her or his actions and words positively affect those around them.

In an interview published by *Bottom Line* magazine, former President Jimmy Carter said this about the virtues of aging:

> *"The most useful, fulfilling thing we can do as we get older is to help others. One of our society's greatest mistakes is the failure to measure, or even acknowledge, the tremendous contribution that older people make."*

Measuring greatness is tremendously challenging. Yet, the assumption of positive effect provides direction. Our respondents believe that the actions of great individuals have positive effects in the lives of others. Hopefully, your striving for greatness will embolden you to make a difference in the lives of others.

Total Humanness
December 2002

Picking up *The New York Times* lately is a painful endeavor. From threats of war and mass destruction, to scandals rocking the political, corporate, and religious world, it seems there are myriad challenges. Those we hoped would lead us through this morass are sinking in quicksand of their own making. Who can provide some sanity and focus?

A recent article on "total leadership" by Stewart Friedman, a Wharton professor, highlights what he believes are characteristics of the leaders we need right now. His ideas parallel our research about greatness, and identify ways to reinforce the importance of these characteristics in our lives. He summarizes leadership this way:, "It boils down to being real, being whole, and being creative."

What surprises us is that he presents total leadership as a "new approach to leadership." Since when did we stop teaching our leaders to have authenticity, integrity, and creativity? That could be part of the problem.

We also note that what Professor Friedman identifies as total leadership, is what we believe is "total humanness." These are strengths that we can have and must develop to deal with today's challenges. How do we develop and reinforce these strengths?

Professor Friedman writes, "Authenticity — being real — arises when individuals behave in ways that are consistent with their core values." In our research, we're intrigued by how often the word "values" arises. Yet, as we identified in "The Assumption of Positive Effect" (November 2002), we often assume positive meaning when it comes to values. How many of us have taken time to identify our core values and examine all aspects of our lives to see if we're being consistent? And what happens when competing demands seem to require different values? Core values allow us to battle the discrepancy with power that comes only through authenticity.

As for being whole Professor Friedman believes, "Integrity — being whole — arises when different aspects of life fit together coherently and consistently." Within the mental health community it's seen as unhealthy for one individual to have multiple personalities. Yet it's often the case that individuals mentally compartmentalize their lives so that each part — work, home, community, themselves — occupies separate areas. Being whole means seeing life as one and being aware that all of the different parts of our lives affect the others. We need a boundary-less concept of our lives. This would involve identifying various aspects of life and tearing down walls we may have created to allow the energy from one part of our life to affect and be affected by the other parts.

Finally, on being innovative, Professor Friedman offers, "Creativity — being innovative — arises when individuals question traditional assumptions and continually experiment with how things are done, courageously embracing and initiating change." We create rituals and habits for ourselves out of the need for efficiency.

Consider this adage: If you always do what you've always done, you'll always get what you always got. Sometimes we need to evaluate the outcome and decide to change it, which requires the strength to identify the issue or challenge. More importantly, it requires permitting ourselves the freedom to try something new.

The issues challenging our world will not disappear without our intervention. Intervention requires grounded, focused individuals who will act with authenticity, integrity, and creativity. Only with total humanness can we deal with difficult issues and transform the pain into possibilities.

The Fear Factor

January 2003

What gets in the way of achieving personal greatness? When we asked that question in a recent survey, "fear" was identified as the primary reason. Our survey respondents identified various fears that affect their journey toward greatness. Some fears are familiar, such as the fear of failure or, conversely, the fear of success. Other fears are more elusive, such as the fear of change (e.g., taking on a new role, or social status). In any case, fear was identified as the primary barrier to realizing potential.

Psychologist Abraham Maslow named fear of greatness the "Jonah Syndrome." He named it the "Jonah Syndrome" based on the biblical figure of Jonah, whose story illustrates how fear keeps us from reaching our potential:

> *"When Jonah is called to be a prophet, he immediately feels fear. Jonah gives into the fear and attempts to run away from his calling. Sailing to a distant land, the ship he boards is caught in a huge storm. Jonah believes he is responsible for the storm and asks that the sailors throw him overboard. Swallowed by a whale, Jonah is vomited up on the shore of the very city that he is supposed to preach in. Almost immediately he converts the entire city. Then he complains because his success has brought different results than he wanted."*
>
> — (Maslow's telling of the Story of Jonah)

Maslow identified fear as the greatest barrier to self-actualization (fulfilling one's potential). We become fearful of possibilities. Fear of discovering "self" immobilizes us. We find ourselves doing "nothing" in order to avoid failure. We suffer from the Imposter Syndrome — the fear of being discovered as far less than what we present ourselves to be. In reality, fear is necessary; it keeps us alive. Our human ability to react to dangerous situations is hard wired. What we've noticed is the unique way that individuals who achieve personal greatness deal with fear. They do not allow it to stop them from doing what they need or want to accomplish.

Maslow was able to identify the fear holding him back. "There is now the possibility of new and higher Eros (self-actualization), but it necessarily brings in its wake the terror of new and subtler Thanatos (death and transformation) … It is … impossible for me to orient meaningfully to life's future because I am terrified of life's present…"

For Maslow, the fear of releasing the present kept him from moving forward into the future. Once he identified this fear, he was able to move further toward his goal of self-actualization.

We are similar to Maslow and Jonah. We have a specific calling that only we can attain. For many of us, the fear factor gets in the way.

What are you afraid of?

Fear Factor II
February 2003

Writing about greatness at this historical moment presents a challenge. Today, threats and increased information about biological, chemical, and nuclear weapons, can make going to the store a difficult decision. Contemplating the fears that inhibit greatness seems a bit grandiose. Yet, after receiving our last newsletter about the "Fear Factor," one survey respondent sent us a story that powerfully reminded her how to deal with her worst fears:

> *"A bird whistling softly on a jungle branch enjoyed the sun and warmth of the day. So engrossed was the bird that she failed to notice the approach of a snake. Turning abruptly, the bird spotted the snake on the branch near enough to see its fangs, but not near enough to prevent her from flying away. But paralyzed with fear, the bird forgot about her power of flight and the ability she had to escape danger."*

Our respondent shared what happened to her after hearing this ancient story. "I bought a primitive little wooden bird on a twig and I hung it in my studio so it would always remind me of the wings I have but often forget about when I become fearful…"

For some, paralysis seems normal in the face of overwhelming odds. We're overwhelmed with negativity and fear in the presence of so much information. We know now more than ever before about dangers that don't necessarily affect us directly. Our natural human reaction is to be fearful when we're not in control. And while this fear makes sense because it warns us of dangers around us, it can also be the start of action-stopping paralysis. Still, there are those who, when confronting the same information, never continue forging ahead in difficult times. What characteristics propel such different reactions to the same circumstances?

First, great individuals tend to overcome fear and the ensuing paralysis by taking action. But remember, individuals smitten by a stroke do not immediately walk around the block. They take small, slow steps that serve to restore their lives and sense of personal power. When confronted with fear, we can overcome paralysis by taking the steps that reassure ourselves and others that we can still participate in life.

Next, great individuals overcome fear by deciding exactly which actions to take in the face of fear. They evaluate their steps in light of their values and goals. Currently, we're hearing from many individuals who are reexamining their lives and asking hard questions about where they want to be and what they want to do. Perhaps the dire circumstances of today's world can inspire us to take steps we might not otherwise take; steps that are more honest, true to our values, and courageous.

Moving forward in the face of fear and the paralysis it can cause, is not foolhardy. At the same time, the opposite of paralysis is not thoughtless movement. Threats provide the opportunity for us to think carefully about our direction and plan accordingly. Each decision and step reminds us that we're in charge of our lives.

Can You Focus?
March 2003

You've probably met those unique individuals who, during a conversation, make you feel special and important. They have a powerful ability to be so present that each exchange contains intensity not found elsewhere. They bring that same intensity and focus to everything they do, thus opening up possibilities seemingly not available to the rest of us.

In our latest survey, respondents identified "lack of focus" as one of the major factors preventing them from achieving personal greatness. Myriad choices, 24/7 information, and constant distraction scattered respondents' energy in many directions.

Single-minded focus is all but entirely lost in American society. Rarely do we do one thing at a time any more. Having been taught to multitask, we somehow believe that we can focus on two or more things simultaneously and do all of them equally well. This is a lie. Yet we persist in holding conference calls while typing emails, reading newspapers while talking with others, trying to do everything with a cell phone up against one ear.

Some individuals have harnessed the power of focus. In the immediate moment they are more present to others, aware of their surroundings, make clear decisions, and seem to enjoy life. They stand out because they don't seem harassed or rushed. They accomplish more with greater calm than the rest of us. How could you obtain this characteristic?

You could begin by challenging yourself to do those things that are important to you one activity at a time. Whether eating dinner with your family, working on a project, or just sitting still, try focusing on being in the moment and becoming aware of what draws you away. What are the most important aspects of what you're doing? How do these affect others?

When you first attempt this, you may find that you're frustrated and thwarted by the static in your head. Gradually, as you persist on focusing, this static will clear and better insights will emerge. You'll find yourself becoming more present in life and work without being pulled every which way by your thoughts.

If you develop the power of focus, what will happen? Your quality of life will immediately improve. Each moment will take on greater significance and if there's someone present, that person will become aware of the moment and your power in it.

You can begin by establishing priorities, focusing on what's most important. You may notice how daily events gain new significance when you allow time to explore all the possibilities of one thing at a time. Most importantly, your life will come alive in new ways.

The Quest
April 2003

After almost two years and hearing from more than 300 regular participants, THE GREATNESS PROJECT is moving in a different direction. We originally began this research effort to identify characteristics of those who, during times of difficulty, would achieve greatness in life and work. Data we've recently collected and conversations at greatness conferences during the past six months have been very revealing. Although the desire for success is still very present, we're discovering a quest for something deeper than public success.

Now, in response, we're shifting our focus to this question: "What are the elements of greatness in human beings?" We're interested in discovering those key characteristics that would make someone want to understand and practice the characteristics of human greatness. We use the word "practice" because 80%-90% of our study participants speak about "growth," "journey," and "the path" when they talk about whether they can achieve greatness.

We're noticing a growing desire to identify something much more powerful than fame, money, or success. Our respondents search for ways they can deepen their self-awareness and these searches mirror many philosophical, psychological, and spiritual paths to becoming a fully integrated human being. Having tried a variety of traditional paths to growth that are, in fact, disconnected from daily life, many of our respondents are now focusing on their own work and relationships to better understand how to achieve greatness.

Unlike Don Quixote de la Mancha, our respondents don't feel that they're attacking windmills or dreaming an impossible dream.

They understand the obstacles of daily life, but seek the path to greatness within their chosen professions while helping those around them. As Cervantes said, their hope is "to add a measure of grace to the world."

So where does this quest lead? There's no easy answer, but we can report a growing concern about questions of significance. Individuals share stories with us about dinners, lunch meetings, and even discussion groups where conversations about greatness occur. Instead of treading the path alone, our participants gather others to help them along the way.

If greatness is not measured in success, fame, or achievement then what are the hallmarks? If an individual is known to be a "great human being" what characteristics would we use to describe them? Can we acquire the characteristics of great humans? If so, how? These are big, complex questions, but many are taking time to ask them and to emulate great human beings, thus trying "to add a measure of grace to the world."

Pause for Reflection

May 2003

Someone recently challenged us by saying that the discussion and pursuit of greatness is narcissistic, self-aggrandizing, egotistical, and focused solely on the interests of the individual. Well, we agree that's true only when there's no thoughtful reflection.

In the absence of contemplation, individuals focus on their own immediate goals and gratification because they have little or no awareness of the larger community. "As soon as human beings started considering themselves the source of the highest meaning in the world and the measure of everything, meaning began to ebb and the stature of [human beings] began to shrink," writes Huston Smith in his *Introduction to the Tao Te Ching*. Once we pause for reflection, we can perceive the larger community and our place in it.

Scanning biographies of great women and men reveals the amount of time they spent in reflection. These individuals charted their course only after examining what it would mean within the context of the larger world. Their movement toward history was not constructed within the narrow confines of what they wanted to accomplish but with consideration to discovering their place or purpose in the world.

The challenge most of us face is twofold; first, we have a warped concept of reflection and second, we believe we lack the time for it. "Reflection" is exactly what the word implies; it's a way of seeing where we are right now. Think about looking in a mirror. Unless you place your nose directly against it, not only do you see yourself, but you also see what surrounds you. Proper reflection, then, mirrors who we are and our place in the larger community.

The most important characteristic of powerful reflection is honesty. Time spent in reflection could be full of misdirected, overly optimistic, self-aggrandizing thoughts. Honest reflection allows the individual to see strengths and weakness, goals and aspirations in the context of the larger community.

What about the challenge of making the time for reflection? While we might long for the luxury of retreat, powerful reflection does not require a trip to the mountain top, sitting in the lotus position, and communing with the divine while incense floats around us. Reflection can take place anywhere. Consider, for example, using that long, tedious commute for reflection instead of talking on the phone or listening to the radio. Time spent, even for a few moments, on who we are and what is important will allow us to better balance our needs while regarding those of the larger world.

An absence of reflection turns us in on ourselves and narrows our vision. True reflection opens our eyes and widens our gaze to see the larger dimensions of life and our place within it, helping us to chart a clearer course toward our fullest potential.

When do you find time for your own reflection?

Do You Feel Lucky?
June 2003

Luck fascinates us and has been an interesting part of our research since we began THE GREATNESS PROJECT. Participants have used the word luck to describe success in their careers, marriages, life, etc. Others have refused to use the word luck, believing that they want to leave little to chance in creating wonderful lives; they are in control. Now, there's new research that reveals why we might believe in luck, yet not leave much to chance.

Richard Wiseman, head of the psychology research department at the University of Hertfordshire, has conducted an eight-year research study about luck. Interviewing thousands of individuals and conducting hundreds of experiments, Wiseman believes that he knows what "causes" luck and what does not. Most importantly, Wiseman states that we can learn to be lucky; it's all about the way we think.

First, Wiseman distinguishes between chance and luck. We all experience chance events, events over which we have no control whatsoever. Many great individuals might attribute up to 50% of their success in life to chance. Wiseman, however, believes that only about 10% of our life can be chalked up to chance; the other 40% is defined by the way we think. Consider these four basic principles from his upcoming book, *The Luck Factor.*

MAXIMIZE CHANCE OPPORTUNITIES

Many of our survey participants have written about chance opportunities (i.e., meeting a life partner, connecting with an influential person at an opportune moment). Opportunities are available on a daily basis. The lucky person adopts a relaxed and open attitude and is willing to notice, create, and act on these opportunities.

LISTEN TO YOUR LUCKY HUNCHES

You've probably been present when someone tried something new and different while reasoning, "I had a hunch." This ability to trust intuition is common to lucky people. They develop intuition through meditation and focus so that they learn to listen to their gut feelings.

EXPECT GOOD FORTUNE

Being around a "Pollyanna" is challenging, yet somehow their lives seem to skirt the disasters that befall so many others. Believing in good fortune is not just a mindset; it translates into behavior. In the face of failure, individuals who expect good fortune persist while others give up. It's a case of self-fulfilling prophecy. They make the good fortune happen because they persevere.

TURN BAD LUCK INTO GOOD

Seeing "the silver lining in the cloud" is not an annoying denial of reality, but based on good psychological techniques to help cope with ill fortune. Upon encountering difficulty, these "lucky" individuals immediately see how things could have been worse, so they move on and take control of the situation.

Some individuals dismiss the successful or joy-filled lives of others by claiming, "They're just lucky." Perhaps there is more truth to that statement than we first thought. Luck seems to be a way of observing and interacting with the world. Based on sound psychological principles, luck allows people to believe fortune will happen to them. They will see new opportunities and act upon them. If an endeavor does not go well, they learn something new and build on that knowledge to be successful elsewhere.

So, we have to ask: do you feel lucky?

Interior Design
July 2003

There's a growing body of evidence that some in the United States are attempting to shift their focus to internal experience. TV reflects a current focus on externals with popular shows such as, "Who Wants To Be a Millionaire?" "Trading Spaces," and "Extreme Makeover." Cosmetics is the fastest growing industry in the United States as the amount of money donated annually to non-profit organizations decreases. Yet, the success of Po Bronson's book *What Should I Do With My Life?* and the proliferation of life coaches indicate a growing movement from an external to an internal focus.

We say that this societal focus on externals is predictable in the absence of direction. When we drift like a rudderless boat, mass media is bound to rule. The good news is that finding a purpose or goal in life is not entirely alien to us. Mostly, we're out of practice.

During childhood, we dream about who and what we'll become. We plan, practice, and hone skills to achieve our dreams whether they are in sports, art, theater, or business. Reaching young adulthood, our dreams are still possible. At that crossroads, a rare few continue to live a fulfilled life by following their life dreams. Others succumb to the pressure of society or the lure of money.

The good news is that we don't completely lose our ability to set goals and dream. We continue to exemplify goal setting at work, and we dream and plan with our children. The bad news is that we often cease working on our own interior design and allow our lives to become captive to entropy, apathy, or atrophy.

As part of THE LEADERSHIP JOURNEY℠ we conduct, we ask individuals to examine their life principles and goals. Few individuals have taken the time to establish why they do what they do and who they really are. Society does not encourage this level of inquiry. When was the last time you asked yourself, "Who (or what) do I want to be when I grow up?" And if you have asked yourself that question, what have you done with the answer?

Chances are, some sort of fear is preventing you from either asking the question or pursuing the answer. Perhaps you fear that if you voice (or write down) your goal, hope, or dream, you will fall woefully short of achieving it. Or, maybe fear arises when you see that you can, in fact, accomplish your dream, but only if you change your current situation. Or, you might be afraid of picking the wrong dream. There are many other fears that keep us from asking who or what we want to be. These fears inhibit us from planning our interior design.

Why should you bother taking the time to identify who and what you want to be?

We find that many who pursue a goal in life, or live according to a greater principle discover that even the mundane moments of their daily lives grow in importance. They can see how these moments are part of a larger picture. Goal or principle-oriented people don't tend to pursue urges simply for the sake of doing something. Instead, they find meaning because they know who they want to be and what they hope to accomplish, or they are in the process of discovery.

In the absence of a goal, any path will do. In the absence of principles, someone will provide it for us. In the absence of real meaning, we seek momentary pleasure. Consider the possibility that your life will be happier, more fulfilled, and more peaceful if you take the time to develop your own interior design and then live according to it.

Put Another Marble in Your Jar
August 2003

We recently presented our research on greatness to a group of managers attending a regional conference. We used a visual metaphor to reinforce the message. Each participant received an empty glass jar. On the tables in front of them were containers of beautiful multicolored marbles; the makings of an amazing mosaic. As we began, many of the managers in the room wondered how the jar and marbles related to the topic of our presentation, "Unleashing The Greatness Within."

Using research from our survey we highlighted qualities of greatness, providing stories and examples about seemingly ordinary lives filled with greatness. Once we established the existence and description of each moment of greatness, we asked if anyone in the room had experienced that quality. One-by-one, time-after-time, every hand in the room went up. After they raised their hands for each quality, we told them to put a marble in their jar. We heard marbles dropping into jars and watched the colors rise.

We then asked managers to describe other qualities of great lives. Many participants shared great moments they had witnessed. Once again, after each example or story, we invited those who had experienced that quality in their own lives to put a marble in their jar.

By now, their jars were half-full. Two realizations dawned on all of us. First, some awakened to the reality that they already had greatness present in their lives. When thinking about greatness, many of us only focus on others and never realize that the same qualities we admire exist in us.

Secondly, as we looked at the empty half of our jars, we realized that our jar is never really full. Each day we determine how our lives will be lived and viewed. We choose the actions and qualities we place in the jar of our lives. Whether we believe the jar expands each day so that we can place more in it, or it's emptied out each night so that each day stands alone, we seek to build a mosaic of encounters and behaviors that enrich us and those with whom we come in contact.

For many this is an important epiphany. Somehow, we tend to believe that we've built our legacy by adulthood and are now mostly finished. Aside from a cataclysmic event, life seems to be settled for many of us. Yet, we hear all the time about midlife crises when individuals do something drastic because, having taken stock of their lives, they don't really like what they see. They dive into radical change to fulfill a dream they always had, or to achieve a dream they now seek.

The shocking truth is that you do not have to create or experience a life changing event to determine the course of your life. Every day, every moment, every encounter presents opportunities to live out your life differently or to build on the legacy you've already begun.

Each and every day you have opportunities to place encounters and behaviors in the unfilled space of your life to build your own mosaic of greatness. Many aspects of greatness are already present in your life.

What piece will you add today?

The Question "Why?"

September 2003

"Why do you do it that way?" "Why don't you try another way?" These two seemingly innocuous questions have the ability to irritate, frustrate, and baffle almost anyone. These inquiries have the power to stop us in our tracks. At our worst, we kill the messenger along with the message and move on. At our best, we pause, consider the questions, and even perhaps change our direction. Questions about why something is done a particular way challenges the status quo.

As adults, we settle into routine very quickly. At home and at work we create successful, efficient processes and then are reluctant to change them. Even successful routines that help us accomplish goals can lull us into inertia if we don't question our current work or life styles. Complacency is easier. The familiar is seductive.

We see an interesting phenomenon as we engage individuals and teams in performance enhancement work. Individuals and teams who display excellence in a particular area tend to be most open to suggestions, questions, and even challenges. They listen carefully to everything that is said, weigh the information and then proceed, sometimes in the same direction or with the same behavior; sometimes taking the suggestion and pursuing another approach.

We're fascinated that the greatest resistance seems to come from individuals and teams who are not close to excellence. Defensiveness abounds as they resist any suggestions or vehemently insist that they're doing all they can.

Carly Fiorina, CEO of Hewlett-Packard said, "One of the things that distinguishes success from mediocrity or failure is the ability to keep learning. You can learn from everything that happens in life and from everyone you come in contact with in life."

Today's media is filled with the mention of "coaches." Executive coaches, life-style coaches, and plain old coaches abound. Everything seems to have its own type of coach. Yet, for all the faddishness there might be an important lesson behind this movement. We often need to be challenged in order to continue growing.

We recently learned this lesson with our business when we hired another consultant to join us. Intelligent and successful, he immediately began asking questions about the way we do things. His questions are always respectful, but they always seem irritating because they challenge our status quo. Either we have to defend the current process, or agree with him and fix it. Change is not easy.

In many ways, he has become our coach and his questions allow us to move toward a higher level of efficiency and productivity. We expect some discomfort and difficulty along the way, but are willing to experience that because we want to continue learning.

Who is your coach? Who asks the difficult questions that propel you to refine your work, your dreams, your life? We don't necessarily have to hire a professional. Children, spouses, friends, and co-workers can play that part in our lives if only we hear them and are open to their inquiries.

"Why?" can be an irritating question, but responding to it can stimulate necessary growth.

Creative Chaos
October 2003

While compiling our latest GREATNESS PROJECT survey results we were fascinated by almost universal responses indicating the desire to imagine, to build, to pursue new ventures, and to love more deeply. This, we believe, is essentially the desire to be creative.

About creativity, psychologist Rollo May has said, "The creative process must be explored as representing the highest degree of emotional health, as the expression of the normal people in the act of actualization of themselves." Many of us don't envision ourselves as creative; we identify creativity with artists, actors, writers, etc. Yet creativity abounds in our day-to-day encounters, our work, and our lives. Opportunities present themselves every moment, whenever we opt to rethink and revise rather than doing it "the way it has always been done."

Many of us envision our creative selves as something left behind in childhood. Now that we are adults, we're afflicted with terminal seriousness. The symptoms of this affliction manifest themselves particularly through an unwillingness to consider new ideas or new ways and a predilection toward the routine. Only when the routine has been utterly demolished through change or calamity do we consider other options.

In reality, our very nature is creative and we frustrate ourselves and deny our own humanity when we inhibit the process. M.C. Richards once wrote, "We have to realize that a creative being lives within ourselves, whether we like it or not, and that we must get out of its way, for it will give us no peace until we do."

If then our very nature cries out to be creative, why do we deny and inhibit creativity? One reason is because creativity is messy. Creativity tosses order aside, scrambles all the pieces of whatever is being considered until there is no semblance of routine and reconstructs everything based on a different view. Essentially some chaos is necessary. "Chaos is a prelude to creativity," writes author and theologian Matthew Fox. "We need to learn, as every artist needs to learn, to live with chaos and, indeed, to dance with it as we listen to it and attempt some ordering."

Yet, our resistance remains because for some of us, age and maturity have numbed our desire to embrace chaos and creativity. How do we return the creativity to our lives? In his book, *Creativity*, Matthew Fox outlines two essential ways we can unleash our natural state of creativity.

LEARN TO PRAISE

Take notice. Routine dulls perceptions and clouds vision. We fail to see how others assist us, how the world nurtures us and we miss possibilities to be grateful. Examining or changing routines at the office or at home forces us to a new level of awareness heightening our ability to thank others or even to acknowledge our own capabilities.

OPEN TO JOY

The opposite of terminal seriousness, joy, becomes natural when we allow ourselves to fully embrace and experience the newness of life that becomes evident when we take notice. Many adults refrain from expressing too much joy, but perhaps we can allow ourselves to smile.

Creativity does not mean that our lives must be lived in chaos, but rather that we learn to become comfortable with the chaos that ensues once we unleash our creativity. Once we allow the chaotic part of the process then we can fully embrace creativity and hope for a fresh, vibrant outcome.

Your Scenic Overlook

November 2003

West of Purcellville, Virginia, Route 7 sharply rises up a small mountain, reaching an apex before plunging into the Shenandoah Valley. At that apex, along the saw-toothed edges of its peaks, runs the Appalachian Trail. Forging onto the trail from Route 7, trees obscure the view and travelers are quickly lost in a world of leaves, rocks, branches, and shrubs with only an occasional blue-dotted tree marking the trail. Any sense of location is obscured until travelers reach Bear's Den, a scenic overlook that reveals the resplendent Shenandoah Valley. The breathtaking view immediately awakens travelers to how far they have come.

Along the journey toward greatness, we can become like those travelers — so focused on process and destination that we lose track of what we've accomplished. Leonardo Da Vinci identified the challenge:

> *"To the ambitious, whom neither the boon of life, nor the beauty of the world suffice to content, it comes as penance that life with them is squandered, and that they possess neither the benefits nor the beauty of the world."*

> — Michael Gelb,
> *How To Think Like Leonardo Da Vinci*

Da Vinci identified the value of stopping for a moment on the journey toward our own potential to realize what we have and how far we have come. It's fitting to realize in this month when we celebrate Thanksgiving, that we can create a scenic overlook for our journey by living in gratitude. Gratitude not only helps us evaluate what we've achieved, but energizes us for the rest of our journey.

Gratitude also has the power to transform the lives of those around us. Imagine being aware of all that others do for us and then expressing gratitude. A powerful connection is created when we acknowledge what others mean to us. In those moments, we connect to a world larger than ourselves.

Gratitude takes the spotlight off us for the moment and places it elsewhere. As self-absorption drops away we become more open to explore new ideas and new concepts.

Try taking a moment, an hour, or even an entire day to notice how far you have come and how blessed you are on your journey toward greatness. Who has helped you along the way?

Gratitude is the scenic overlook that allows us to review our accomplishments and gives us the energy to move on.

The Spirituality of Achieving Greatness
December 2003

Compartmentalizing helps us maintain focus during difficult times. We walk through the front door of our home and relegate work's challenging moments to a corner of consciousness, thereby allowing us to enjoy family time. Conversely, we tend to focus on work when other areas of life challenge us. And yet, this survival skill can lead to fragmentation.

Nowhere else is this fragmentation more evident than in the relationship between our spiritual and work worlds. By establishing the separation of church and state, the United States officially excluded religion from government and our governing. This separation seems to have so permeated all areas of our lives that today many of us equate spirituality with religious practice; we certainly differentiate it from work.

We want to note, however, the growing trend toward realizing how personal development, work, and spirituality are intertwined in every moment. Today, we can find books that reference spirituality in the workplace. Indeed, our own research has revealed a perceived link between spirituality and striving to achieve greatness.

On a recent survey we asked, "Do you believe there is a spiritual dimension to attempting to achieve your greatness?" We expected some individuals would reply, "Yes." We were overwhelmed when 100% of our respondents agreed that there's a spiritual dimension to the greatness quest.

In *The Art of Happiness*, the Dalai Lama noted, "I believe that it's essential to appreciate our potential as human beings and recognize the importance of inner transformation. Sometimes, I call this having a spiritual dimension in our life."

He continued by explaining that there are two levels to the spiritual dimension. One is directly associated with religious beliefs and the other, which he believes is more important, has to do with our shared humanity displayed as compassion, caring, goodness, kindness, and the like. This *basic* spirituality, as the Dalai Lama calls it, is what everyone can practice daily to draw us closer to each other and also to release our inner potential.

Our study concurs with the Dalai Lama. As we find ways to participate in our shared humanity and develop the characteristics of compassion etc., we are forced to develop internally; this assists our movement toward greatness. Daily activity can drive inner transformation. Striving toward inner transformation is one way we explore spirituality.

There's another way we become aware of spirituality as we strive toward greatness. This happens when, as we explore inner resources, tap hidden potential, and discover personal gifts, we acknowledge that there's something greater, something beyond us toward which we strive.

Every time we attempt to develop core gifts or help others develop theirs, we dance with the spiritual nature of our beings. This spiritual dance occurs daily in our homes, jobs, and the rest of our lives, not separate but an essential part of who we are — and who we can become. Spirituality is another characteristic that demands exploration on our journey to achieving greatness.

Being Where You Are
January 2004

"Do you think individuals can unleash their greatness in a corporate setting?" This question, posed to us on the Internet radio show, "Invent The Future" (aired 12/22/04), prompted us to reflect on a larger question: Does the place we work help or hinder whether we will be able to attain our personal greatness?

Initially, we believed that living our personal values might be more challenging to accomplish in a corporate environment. We thought achieving personal greatness might be easier when individuals pursued their own business, or worked in a non-corporate setting. However, participants in our most recent survey did not agree. We asked, "Do you believe you can achieve your potential in your current place of employment?" Two-thirds of those working in corporate environments believe they can achieve their greatness in that work setting.

Being in an ideal situation of our choosing seems to create the strongest possibility of achieving personal greatness. Yet, why is it that some in seemingly "ideal" situations fail to achieve anything? Conversely, others still move toward personal greatness in settings that are less than ideal. How do they shine when their work environment strives to hinder them from their personal goal(s)?

There are no simple answers, yet some important concepts may help you continue on the journey. Two concepts bear special consideration.

First, the journey to personal greatness is an inner path; blaming external situations saps energy and wastes time. Changing external realities may help, but at the end of the day, we either develop ourselves or we do not. Jon Kabat-Zinn captures this concept very well in his book, *Wherever You Go There You Are* when he writes:

> *"It's easier and less threatening to our sense of self to project our involvement in our problems onto other people and the environment. It's so much easier to find fault, to blame, to believe that what is needed is a change on the outside, an escape from the forces that are holding you back, preventing you from growing from finding happiness. This way of thinking and seeing is an all-too-prevalent trap. There is no successful escaping from yourself in the long run, only transformation."*

Transformation cannot occur if we focus only on changing the world around us believing that will bring happiness and fulfillment. Focusing first on our development gives us the power to eventually change the realities around us.

Secondly, how can remaining in difficult situations help us achieve greatness? Jon Kabat-Zinn writes:

> *"The challenge is to work with the very circumstances that you find yourself in — no matter how unpleasant, how discouraging, how limited, how unending and stuck they may appear to be — and to make sure that you have done everything in your power to use their energies to transform yourself before you decide to cut your losses and move on."*

Whether working in a corporation or a home, having the ideal life, or struggling where we are and with what surrounds us, will not determine our journey to personal greatness. Only what we do with what we're given, how we learn from it and move on, will create the legacy of a great life.

The Inner Devil
February 2004

A barrier confronts many of us as we attempt to grow, change, or be creative. Pondering options, our mind veers into "catastrophizing." Almost immediately, we imagine the worst possible outcomes, suspecting that dire consequences will result from our actions. Fearing the negative repercussions of trying something new, we often reverse course or remain stuck in our current state, unwilling to risk the "inevitable" downside.

In our GREATNESS PROJECT surveys, we've found that 90% of our respondents identify fear — either fear of success or fear of failure — as what inhibits achieving personal greatness. All our respondents live productive, successful lives and strive to move forward into a future of their own making. And yet this destructive fear arises to inhibit their growth.

For decades, psychologists have reveled in addressing this phenomenon. Naming it the "judge," "parent," or "naysayer," psychologists have focused on the inner voice that inhibits creativity, devalues us, or fosters visions of catastrophic failure. What is this inner voice? We want to weigh into the discussion and name it the "DEVIL." Now before you think we've gone over the edge, let us explain.

As we explore what inhibits individuals from achieving personal greatness, we generally discover negative and destructive self-talk. This negativity bubbles up whenever they confront change or need to make a life decision; it drives their fear. Yet most of the time, these internal conversations defy reality. Destructive self-talk minimizes or entirely ignores life achievements. We posit that the impediment to greatness happens when we allow the D.E.V.I.L. to take over because we "Deny Everything Valid In Life."

When we, at a moment of decision-making, choose to ignore times when we've successfully changed, we deny our experiences and their validity. When we come to a crossroads and immediately think about the worst possible outcomes of deciding, we deny lessons we've learned through success and failure alike. Most of all, when we somehow believe we cannot change in the face of difficult conditions, we ignore the fact that we've already made successful changes throughout our lives.

Those who move toward greatness identify this negative inner voice. They don't ignore it, but instead listen for it. They listen carefully for the irrational thought processes that expose the D.E.V.I.L. within. Successful individuals then repel the onslaught of disastrous premonitions by remembering a life of challenges met and obstacles overcome. Using valid life experiences allows them to continue moving successfully toward new goals.

What happens when you try to achieve new things? Many of us have not identified our D.E.V.I.L. We listen carefully to this strange inner voice without holding it accountable. The next time you choose to change your life, strive for something new, or strike out in a new direction, listen to your inner voice. Bring the dark thoughts into the bright spotlight of reality. Recall your life of successful change and allow those thoughts to counteract irrational fear so you can move forward to new goals and achievements.

Scott Asalone & Jan Sparrow

Measuring Success
March 2004

A recent *USA Today* poll indicates that 64% of those surveyed hate their jobs, yet when compared with almost any other nation, Americans spend more time at work. Our country maintains one of the highest standards of living, and yet we're among the most dissatisfied with our lives. We continue to work harder, and yet professional success eludes us. Yes, we live out the curse of Sisyphus, expending great effort to push that proverbial boulder up the mountain, only to have it roll down again whenever we nearly reach the top.

Why do many of us accept this overemphasis on work as we pursue success? Possibly because historical accounts of those who have achieved greatness often focus on their single-minded pursuit of goals to the exclusion of anything else. Success stories generally tend to gloss over personal sacrifices. And so, this notion of single-minded pursuit to achieve success is the standard of behavior expected of achievers. This is particularly true in corporate America where personal needs are readily relinquished to achieve higher goals.

We're pleased to report that new research reveals how it's possible to take a more balanced approach to evaluate and attain professional — and personal — success.

In a *Harvard Business Review* article, "Success That Lasts" (March 2004), Laura Nash and Howard Stevenson identify four components of enduring success. Their research reveals how high achieving individuals tend to develop the capacity to balance their lives so they can succeed in each of these four categories:

Happiness — feelings of pleasure and contentment about life.

80

Achievement — accomplishments that compare favorably against similar goals of others.

Significance — the sense of making a positive impact on cherished people.

Legacy — establishing values or accomplishments that help others find future success.

Nash and Stevenson suggest taking the time to jot down what constitutes success for self, family, work, and community within each of these categories. At this point, you might feel overwhelmed, believing that you can't possibly succeed in all these categories. Yet we've discovered that evaluating life and work according to these four categories can serve to motivate you. We advocate acknowledging the success you've generated already, and then identifying areas that need to be balanced or filled in.

The final and most important contribution of this research is "the reasoned pursuit of just enough." Nash and Stevenson discovered that people experience real satisfaction through "the deliberate imposition of limits." The successful people they studied "were able to focus intensely on one task until it gave them a particular sense of satisfaction, then put it down and jump to the next category with a feeling of accomplishment and renewed energy."

Clearly, we cannot push the proverbial boulder up the mountain each day without a break. Balancing all four components — happiness, achievement, significance, and legacy — will help us understand the success we already have and rejuvenate ourselves to continue pursuing greatness.

Pass It On
April 2004

Turning on the television or picking up a recent newspaper takes courage. Bad news easily overwhelms anything positive we might hear or read. Solitude seems a safe option in the face of these stories about violence, retribution, jealousy, hatred, greed, or envy. Forging ahead through daily negative bombardment can be a gargantuan task. How can we help others attain greatness while surrounded by such depressing news?

Helping others attain greatness is a responsibility that respondents to our recent GREATNESS PROJECT survey shoulder quite willingly. One hundred percent of our respondents told us they can and want to help others achieve full potential. The question arises, how do they plan to do that? We'd like to suggest one way to help people believe they're capable of something different, something better: Tell a good story.

Storytelling is emerging as a training technique in corporations. Leaders know that telling stories is an effective way to convey ideas. A good story provides the "how to" and "why to" all in one. Many of us learn and are empowered when we hear about greatness in action. We tend to believe that if someone else can succeed, then maybe we can also.

Seventy-eight percent of our respondents acknowledged the value of hearing stories about greatness in others to understand how they can achieve their own greatness. We say that greatness involves encouraging others with the good stories.

Here's an example of how this can work. Two weeks ago, we had the luxury of staying at the Ritz Carlton in Laguna Nigel, California while speaking at a conference. We were so enamored with the hotel and its incredible staff that we asked the front desk manager how they maintained such a high level of excellence. "We tell stories about each other," she replied with a smile. She elaborated by revealing that all Ritz Carlton employees at every hotel are encouraged to tell stories to management and staff about fellow employees who provide exceptional client service. Each month these stories are collected and retold to the entire staff. As a result, five employees are selected to receive a "Five Star" badge of honor they wear for the month, plus a cash bonus. The manager added that hearing the stories was the most important part of the program because "we learn great service from each other."

Stories can enhance the possibility of achieving greatness. Think about stories that have encouraged you. Your catalyst may have been the story of a parent or grandparent who overcame incredible odds to succeed. A story about someone famous may have helped you realize you were not so different and inspired you to try something new. One of our survey respondents offered, "The information [about greatness] can be shared with those in our lives. Everyone can benefit from greatness, and it can become contagious." Stories have power to change belief systems, provide examples, and illustrate possibilities.

Each day, bad news can smother dreams and desires by painfully reminding us of the challenges we face to achieve our potential. Telling good stories is a powerful antidote, encouraging others to continue developing. When you hear or witness a story about greatness, pass it on.

Pride Goeth Before Greatness
May 2004

"Pride goeth before a fall" is a Biblical proverb many of us encountered during our developmental years. We think a more intricate perspective underlies the broad statement. Over the past three years, we've noticed how the great individuals and companies we've studied share a foundational belief. All have pride in themselves and their accomplishments. This is not an arrogant belief that they're untouchable or unaccountable to anyone, but a sense that they and their work are worthwhile.

Great individuals manifest pride in how they value themselves and their work. Because work is a manifestation of who they are, they take special care to deliver exceptional service or value because they have to deliver the best. Our finest example of this ethos is Sammy, who worked at the Sunoco gas station in Ewing, New Jersey. Sammy treated customers as if they were driving up to the Ritz.

When we first interviewed him, Sammy told us, "If anyone leaves my gas station and is not happier than when they arrived, I failed." So committed was he to servicing each customer that we initially thought he owned the gas station. His contribution was magnified in our eyes when we realized that he simply pumped gas and dispensed the finest service around. There was always a line at the station and it was because of Sammy.

We recently dropped by the Sunoco station just to see Sammy, only to discover he's no longer employed there. We were told that one customer was so impressed with his dignity and service that he offered Sammy a better job. Sammy's pride in himself paid off.

Corporations and companies generate emotional reactions from their employees. When this reaction is pride in the organization, individuals manifest their pride—or sense of positive ownership — in the consistent positive, proactive behavior they pour on their customers or into their work. They want their company to maintain its positive reputation and will do everything in their individual power to make it happen.

We experienced the power of pride while delivering a developmental session to Metropolitan Museum of Art employees. We were stunned by the length of service most of them held. When questioned why they stayed, they told us about their respect for the institution and their desire to see it persevere. They regaled us with story after story about the museum's success, sounding like parents bragging with pride. And their pride revealed itself in how they wanted to learn how to create an even better environment.

Similar pride was manifest to us at the Westin Grand Bohemian Hotel in Orlando, Florida. This amazing hotel is an absolute jewel with an art collection distributed throughout and a Bösendorfer grand piano in the lobby. Employees' pride is revealed in the care they take with each guest and the passion they exude when asked about the hotel.

Perhaps we need to nuance the phrase "Pride goeth before the fall" to "Pride precedes greatness, arrogance goes before the fall." Sammy's pride in himself created more opportunities for him to excel. The Met continues to be the number one tourist attraction in New York City. And the Westin Grand Bohemian Hotel has won the Best Service Award two years running and its employees were quick to tell us that they want to win the award again this year.

Moving Beyond Your "Set Point"
June 2004

To some, meeting individuals who are perpetually happy is at best, amusing; at worst, downright irritating. Why are these people so happy? Don't they understand that life and work are serious? Either we validate our umbrage by identifying our life or work as more important than theirs, or we consider them "dolts" and move on. A closer look reveals that happiness is both genetically determined and developed intentionally. So, it's possible to actively create a more satisfying, productive life.

Sonja Lyubomirsky, Ph.D. at the University of California, developed a model to explain the balance of genetics vs. discipline in creating happiness. Her work confirms the research finding that approximately 50% of happiness is genetic. At birth, we acquire an emotional base or happiness "set point." Life variables may cause a momentary rise in happiness, but without additional stimulation we tend to return to our set point. For example, research on lottery winners revealed that although happiness peaked when they won, it returned to its normal set point for happiness after six months. So is our happiness forever stuck at our genetic set point? Not totally, reports Sonja.

An additional 10% of our happiness is influenced by life circumstances such as age, sex, income, and occupation. For example, if you receive a promotion your happiness level will rise above your set point. However, the promotion eventually becomes a normal part of life and happiness returns to its set point. Sonja notes that as humans we become inured to new circumstances as they become routine. Again, major rises or declines in happiness last briefly before happiness returns to where it was prior to the event.

What does the remaining 40% of happiness depend upon? Sonja identified this percentage as "intentional activities." These daily activities, which either boost or deplete the happiness level, are within our control. For example, taking time to do something positive on a regular basis, or being present for a loved one contributes to a rise in happiness. (For other intentional activities see: www.authentichappiness.com) Sonja discovered that variation is key. To avoid numbing the effect of the happiness, we must vary any of these intentional activities, even if only slightly.

Most importantly, if we want to be happy over the course of our lives we have to work at it. There are no short cuts. Like physical fitness, happiness requires diligent maintenance. Many of us have developed "terminal seriousness," the strain of which is revealed in our voices and on our faces. While part of our happiness is genetically predetermined, much of it's up to us. Engaging in daily positive activities will add up to a lifetime of mental fitness. Do this and your life will become so creative, productive, and satisfying that you won't care if your happiness irritates others!

What intentional activities do you engage in to raise the level of your happiness?

Can You See the Gorilla?
July 2004

Howard Schultz took his love of coffee and turned it into a global business when he created Starbucks. How did he do that? It was "impossible thinking."

Some people are able to see things differently than the rest of us. They look at the world, their work, and themselves with clear eyes, not clouded with preconceived notions or ideas. Their clarity lets them find new ways to address problems and identify possibilities. Without the encumbrance of mental models and limited awareness they think of things others believe are impossible. We all have mental models; they are the way we envision the world working. These mental models have a dramatic impact on our business and personal lives. Most of the time what we see and act upon is more a product of what is inside our heads than in the world.

Neurologist Walter Freeman has discovered that whatever information our senses provide stops at the cortex. That sensory information stimulates an internal pattern the brain then uses to "represent" the external situation. So, we see what's already present in our mind. Apparently, Native Americans did not see the first tall ships of European settlers because the image was outside of their mental model; they only saw the smaller boats coming ashore.

Our mental models provide a safe and organized way to categorize what goes on around us so we can understand and interact with our environment. But, mental models can also restrict our ability to process new ways of thinking. They create "tunnel vision" so we only see what we want while possibly missing new, creative ideas.

In a recent study on memory and perception, subjects were

asked to watch a video and count the number of times players with white shirts passed around a basketball. Most of the subjects reported a fairly accurate number of passes, but only 42% saw something even more important: someone wearing a black gorilla costume walking right into the center of the action, beating his chest, and moving off camera. More than half the subjects were so engrossed in counting passes they couldn't see the gorilla.

Gorillas, then, symbolize new ideas. Not seeing them signals a mind stuck in familiar patterns. Impossible thinking can be uncertain and risky, which is why most people avoid it. But it also provides new ways of thinking that allow us to go beyond familiar ideas.

In a new book, *The Power of Impossible Thinking*, Jerry Wind and Colin Crook identify steps we can take to achieve impossible thinking.

- Become explicitly aware of why you see the world the way you do and what that implies.
- Test the relevance of your current mental models against the changing environment.
- Generate new models (if needed) and develop a portfolio of models.
- Overcome inhibitors to change by reshaping the infrastructure (external or personal) that supports the old models.
- Generate and act on new models by experimenting and continuing to assess and strengthen your models.

We invite you to reflect on these questions: Is there a gorilla in front of you that remains invisible? What prevents you from impossible thinking?

First Born Greatness

August 2004

Most families plan for the best for their children, but are often disappointed. Most schools desire greatness in their students, yet few attain it. Most businesses hope for greatness from their employees, but fail to receive it. What allows greatness to develop?

As we work with teams and leaders around the country, we hear individuals say they can't do their best work. The reasons they give usually fall into one of three categories: either their boss or supervisor doesn't truly believe in their potential; or no new opportunities are offered; or (what we hear frequently) they don't receive any feedback. Each factor taken separately can have a negative impact on performance; in combination, they're disastrous. In fact, there's research that suggests managers have a significant role to play in fostering greatness in employees.

Dr. Thomas K. Connellan, former research associate and program director at the University of Michigan, has discovered three keys that unlock peak performance in individuals.

First, he focused on successful first born children, comparing them with those located elsewhere in the birth order. When he quickly discovered genetics was not a key factor in predicting success, he turned his attention to environmental factors. Eventually, he isolated three factors that contribute to the success of firstborn children. He further discovered that individuals respond with greater success when these factors play a role in home, school, and business environments.

What are these factors?

• Positive expectations

- Increased responsibility
- More feedback

When provided together, these factors offer individuals the optimal possibility for success. Sadly, our study reveals that people often struggle under negative expectations, learned helplessness, and little or no feedback at all. Personal greatness is much more achievable when even one of these factors is present.

Positive expectations involve providing more than "rah-rah" encouragement. Dr. Connellan says that you have to really believe that the individual can succeed, you can't fake it. Indeed, positive expectations need to be communicated authentically and regularly.

Individuals grow through the challenge of **increased responsibility**, yet what leaders call empowerment is often abandonment. New responsibilities cannot be heaped on anyone without direction or guidance. The possibility for success is enhanced when information and guidance accompany new responsibilities.

Providing **more feedback** is essential. Individuals succeed when they know what they do well and how they could do better. The tragedy is that often individuals receive no feedback at all. Dr. Connellan argues that a total lack of feedback is even worse than bad feedback, because the individual feels abandoned.

These three simple factors can change the success of individuals in families, schools, and companies. Are these present in your environment?

Positive Expectations
September 2004

When was the last time you attempted something new and those around you were equally convinced that you could achieve your aspirations? Having others believe you can — and will — succeed leads to greater success; their belief strengthens you.

In last month's GREATNESS PROJECT article, we noted research by Dr. Thomas K. Connellan identifying three factors that help people achieve success: positive expectations, increased responsibility, and more feedback. Finding these three factors especially present in first-born children, Connellan discovered these factors accounted for success not found in those born elsewhere in the birth order. He then educated leaders in various environments about these three factors to ascertain whether he could raise success rates of individuals when these factors were present, and found he could. This month, we'll take a deeper look at the first of the three factors, positive expectations.

Environments where expectations are positive create confidence for individuals within them. Confidence tends to build confidence; winners tend to win, and individuals who have people believing in them live up to expectations.

In the 1980's, a well-known study revealed what happened when a group of educators were told they were teaching high achieving children who were, in fact, considered underachievers. A matched group of educators were told they were teaching underachievers when, actually, they were teaching high achievers. At the end of the study, the group of so-called underachievers posted greater success than the high achievers. Why? Because the teachers treated them differently. The teachers' positive expectations manifested itself in their students' success.

Don't we all have high expectations for our children, our co-workers, and ourselves? Yes. And there's an important difference between high expectations and positive expectations.

Many corporate environments have high expectations for employees. In the era of "doing more with less" employees are expected to do the work of two, three, or four employees. These days, the high expectations are that employees do more work. Inherent in positive expectations, however, is the absolute belief that individuals can achieve greater things. When employees receive positive expectations they tend to live up to them.

One of our favorite examples is what happens on the first day of training at Ritz Carlton Hotels. New employees are told, "You are a gift to the organization." The managers mean it and the employees become it.

Imagine an environment where individuals are expected to thrive, not just to survive; to be creative; to go beyond mediocrity to achieve greatness. Such positive expectations would foster powerful, creative people.

Perhaps we can achieve greatness by having positive expectations of ourselves without waiting for environments around us to change. Let's get personal for a moment. As we age, many of us temper our enthusiasm for new adventures to protect our egos. Not wanting to fail, we talk about trying but don't really believe we can succeed. Or, having borne "the whips and scorns of time" (Shakespeare) we rest in the comfort of past achievements and watch in awe as a few others reach new heights we thought unreachable. New possibilities can be fostered by our own positive expectations. As Henry Ford said, "Whether you think you can or you think you can't, you are right."

Greater Responsibility
October 2004

In August's GREATNESS PROJECT article, we noted research by Dr. Thomas K. Connellan that identifies three factors that help people achieve success: positive expectations, increased responsibility, and more feedback. This month, we'll take a deeper look at the second factor: greater responsibility.

Imagining greater responsibility, most of us would groan aloud. We have plenty to do without placing more on top of our current commitments. Yet as we consult with work teams and individuals around the country, we ask two questions. First, "Are you too busy?" The answer is always "yes." Second, "Could you do more?" Surprisingly the answer is almost always "yes."

Most people feel that their strengths are not being used, yet their days are filled with tasks. For each of us to grow into our own greatness, we have to accept greater opportunities to stretch. This is uncomfortable, challenging and taxing, yet there's no better way to learn our limitations and our possibilities.

When interviewed on National Public Radio, jazz musician Branford Marsalis said that he accepts opportunities to play classical music with orchestras because it makes him realize how much he does not know. He accepts the responsibility of learning a different type of music because he believes he can learn from it. Stepping into greater responsibility allows us to identify growth opportunities and capitalize on them.

Where have you accepted new responsibility as an opportunity to grow? Most of us content ourselves with the present workload and are wary of anything that adds to that load. Individuals who seek to develop themselves and succeed in greater and greater arenas, willingly accept or even explore new opportunities to try new things. Individually, we can establish a pattern of growth for ourselves by accepting greater responsibility in a reasonable and responsible way and learning from it.

We can also help others reach greater heights by providing them with more responsibility as a way to learn. In business, the word "empowerment" has reached almost mythological status among the concepts tossed around. But, empowerment can become abandonment when individuals are given new opportunities without the training or the support to succeed. Training and support are essential for individuals to have the opportunity to grow into more responsibility and learn from it.

One tactic used in the military is an especially helpful debriefing technique that can reveal what, if anything, was learned. Note that this technique does not focus on blame (if something went wrong), but rather focuses on what was learned. In military lingo, these are known as AARs (After Action Reviews). When something occurs (positively or negatively) in an engagement, everyone involved is asked these questions.

- What was supposed to happen?
- What did happen?
- What accounts for the difference?
- What can we learn?

Discussing new experiences with others, or helping others debrief their new experiences creates learning in an environment that focuses on growth, not on blame. More responsibility, as Dr. Connellan discovered, can augment the growth of an individual, especially if those involved help him or her to recognize what they learned and grow from it.

More Feedback

November 2004

For the past three months we've been exploring Dr. Thomas K. Connellan's research about three environmental conditions that help people achieve success: positive expectations, increased responsibility, and more feedback. This month, we focus on the positive impact of more feedback.

Imagine a world without any feedback. What if all your work, all the love and care you showed someone else, and every attempt you made to help yourself and others were met with total silence. Imagine if you had absolutely no idea if anyone recognized or cared about what you'd done. The impact of that silence would be depleting, if not totally devastating. Yet, many of us strive to perform our best under work conditions devoid of feedback. Without feedback about our progress, we will not achieve even a fraction of what we are capable, Dr. Connellan says.

How can this new information foster individual growth? Initially, we have to recognize our own need for feedback. The Gallup Organization recently conducted a poll asking successful individuals whether they needed feedback to do a good job. Only 60% replied that they did.

Surprised, researchers followed up with another question about whether respondents believed they performed better when they received feedback and encouragement. This time, 98% replied that they performed better. We have to recognize our need for positive feedback and then surround ourselves with those who will provide it.

At the same time, we can encourage others to do their best by providing encouragement for all they attempt to do. Whether in personal relationships or on the job, we need to let others know what they are doing right. We cannot — and should not — assume: "I don't need to tell them they are doing great, they already know." In fact, when we provide the recognition and encouragement, others are inspired to do great work.

It's even more important to offer the most useful feedback possible. Many of us mistakenly believe that our greatest area of weakness offers the greatest possibility for growth. We reason that if we desire growth, we ought to encourage others to point out our weaknesses. But, author Marcus Buckingham in *Now, Discover Your Strengths*, suggests we stay focused on what we do well, so that we can excel in that area. His research suggests that focusing on strengths and receiving feedback specifically related to them, helps accentuate those strengths and encourages excellence in those areas.

Two other books, *Encouraging the Heart* by James Kouzes and Barry Posner, *and How Full Is Your Bucket* by Tom Rath, zoom in on growth in life and work as a result of receiving positive feedback. These authors also encourage us to provide positive feedback to others. Since we mirror what we receive, this is something we must consciously do, especially since few of us receive any praise or recognition for our own achievements.

If you think this is an overstatement, consider the fact that a 2003 Gallup survey revealed that 40% of employees never received recognition for a job well done; another 40% said they never received recognition at all. Amazingly, 50% of managers admitted never providing feedback for employees. It's really very simple: no feedback leads to minimal growth.

A simple "thank you" or "congratulations on a job well done" goes a long way. But providing an environment where feedback, mostly positive and consistently delivered, allows everyone to move toward greatness.

Generosity
December 2004

In *A Christmas Carol*, Jacob Marley's ghost stands remorseful before Ebenezer Scrooge who attempts to console Marley by saying, "But Jacob, you were always a good man of business." Marley's reply is powerful and sets the underpinning for the whole play as he cries, "Mankind was my business." Scrooge's redemption comes when he realizes that although he had the means to help others, he was lacking in generosity. This time of year generally lends itself to self-reflection, particularly relative to generosity which our research participants noted is a key characteristic of greatness.

What survey participants identify as generosity is the willingness to help others in myriad ways and, in the process, help them move toward greatness.

This past year, some marvelous individuals surprised us with their generosity. For example, on December 12, after winning the Target World Challenge, Tiger Woods donated the entire winner's purse of $1.25 million dollars to his foundation to help educate children. Cynics might dismiss this as a tax deduction for Tiger and miss the point: that Tiger Woods established this foundation and devotes his extra time helping children. It's not just about money.

Possibilities for generosity are endless and need not be done in such a grand manner. Recently, a friend related something that happened to her at Newark Airport. Heading for a flight in Terminal C, she was stopped by a couple who were, to her eye, foreign and obviously lost. Immediately, they began speaking to her in Spanish.

She told us that she was able to understand they were looking for a gate. When she asked to see their tickets, she realized they were in the wrong concourse and only had to walk to the next one. Using a mixture of Spanish, English, and gestures she redirected them to their gate. When we commented on the story with admiration, she replied, "I should have walked them to the gate." She wanted to do more even than she did.

Generosity, when viewed as a characteristic of greatness, is not convenient, self-aggrandizing, and time-bound. Individuals who share this characteristic reflect it in everything they do. In every interaction with others they seek to give and help others in any way they can. Though this might seem to be part of their very nature, it's a discipline.

Our DNA provides plenty of fail-safe mechanisms to protect ourselves, but few to help others. As a discipline, generosity can indeed be developed by beginning with an increased awareness of others. Next, generosity challenges the giver to provide for another's need without subtly making the other subservient. Keeping a keen eye on pride is essential to being generous because pride can surface from being the "giver" or having the means to give. The key is in learning to experience how, in the giving, there's often even more that we receive. Finally, being aware of others gradually allows awareness to grow in all areas of one's life.

Three spirits enlightened Scrooge to the realization that he could help others. Each year, we have a season to remind us of one of the most important characteristics of greatness; generosity.

Finding Your Purpose
January 2005

The question, "Why are you here?" might elicit the memory of a boring philosophy class or the beginning of a long sermon. Still, how we answer this question has a profound impact on our life, our motivation, and our sense of self.

Examine the lives of great individuals and you'll find they are filled with purpose. Their lives are energized and pulled relentlessly toward a goal that infuses everything they do.

We need to be useful; we want to know that our life matters. Yet too often, we lose ourselves in busy lives, then wonder where the years went and what we were trying to accomplish. Identifying our purpose, no matter what our age, gives our life direction, meaning, and power.

The work of identifying life purpose, whether at home or work can be a great challenge. One school of thought suggests that we have to "discover" our purpose, as though it's hidden somewhere in the universe. Our job is to find it, otherwise it will waste away. This implies that someone or something decides our purpose and hides it for us to find. This might seem comforting: we don't have to take full responsibility for our purpose in life, it was given to us.

A second school of thought suggests that we all have gifts and abilities to do something purposeful in this world. Free will confers upon us the immensely powerful responsibility and burden of identifying how we will affect the world around us. Essentially, we decide our purpose and take full responsibility for living it out. This concept is much more challenging, yet also much more freeing.

We can discern our purpose by meditating on these questions:

"What do I have to offer?" and "Where can I make an impact?" Yet in the final analysis, understanding our life purpose is something we sense. It's instinctive and intuitive. Discovering our purpose in life requires us to search with our heart and soul.

As we ponder our life purpose, we need to consider the question, "How can I affect the world a little at a time?" We might like to change the world on a grand scale, but it's more likely that we will have a more modest impact. Robert Kennedy said, "Few of us will have the greatness to bend history itself, but each of us can work to change a small portion of events... It's from numberless acts of courage and belief that human history is shaped."

In December, we were flying back from our last trip of 2004. The flight had been delayed for three hours, cancelled, and reinstated when we finally boarded. Most of the passengers and flight attendants were surly. Carol, our flight attendant, was different. She defused most of the anger with her smile and attentiveness, even getting many of us to laugh. During the flight, when we questioned her about how she was able be so gracious in difficult circumstances she replied, "There is so much anger in the world; I just try every day to bring in some happiness."

"What is our purpose in life?" Understanding our life purpose draws us closer each day to fulfilling that purpose, while also linking daily events toward a significant goal. "The great and glorious masterpiece of [humanity] is how to live with purpose," offered Michel de Montaigne. The question of purpose invites us to examine why we are here and, more importantly, what we will leave for others when we're gone.

Recharging the Batteries
February 2005

It happens mostly when we least expect it, or when it's most inconvenient. Yet, we accept as a reality of modern life that at some point we'll have to recharge the battery on our cell phone or on another technological convenience. We know that without time out for recharging, it will lose its ability to function. Why are we so reluctant to apply this principle of technology to our own life?

We are a nation of movers and shakers, rarely stopping to rest. A recent article in *The New York Times* notes that US employees hand back $21 billion of unused vacation time each year. In 2002, dual income couples with children worked a combined 91 hours a week. With all this perpetual motion, it's little wonder that our "batteries" run out. The accidents, illnesses, and mistakes that happen as a result cost US businesses $300 billion a year.

The physical cost of running on empty is growing. Stress is rampant. According to a recent Gallup poll, 60% of employees surveyed feel overwhelmed by the amount of work they have to do. Still, we continue to do more in the name of efficiency and productivity. Some of us even bring cell phones and laptops on vacation, somehow believing that we can rest *and* be productive.

While physical rest is important, a much more important benefit comes from taking time out for self. Contemplating life, work, and purpose leads to creative and powerful thinking. Though we may not have the wherewithal to take a year of reflection at a Walden Pond like Henry David Thoreau, we can — and should — schedule time each day for reflection.

Creativity especially needs reflective time. The mind demands an alternative path before it will divest itself of a particular way of doing something. And so, creativity within life and work relies on time to think about new pathways. Patterns of habitual behaviors and ways of thinking cannot be broken without reflection.

Reflection is rejuvenating. When we "put our head down and get to work" we tend to lose sight of where we're going and why. Daily tasks become mind-numbing and tedious, losing their meaning. Taking time to reflect on the purpose of our life and work allows us to reengage with fierce determination and clear direction.

Most of us do not have the luxury to reflect for days, let alone weeks, but we must make a good faith effort to devote some time to this essential activity. Without taking time for reflection, we endanger the very things we attempt to build. We need to make time to recharge our batteries. Our pursuit of greatness depends on doing so.

People First
March 2005

In the play "A Man of No Importance," Alfie's dream of producing Oscar Wilde's "Salome" in 1964 Dublin sets off an avalanche of events that challenge and change everyone connected with St. Imelda's Social Hall. Thus, author Terrance McNally reminds us of this crucial reality: we are intimately connected with everyone we encounter; we affect them and they affect us.

Though seemingly obvious, this truism is often obscured in the rush toward success and individualism. In our drive to achieve greater status and acquire more possessions we may ignore the effect we have on friends, family, and co-workers. When it comes to achieving personal greatness, developing an awareness of our interconnectedness not only brings balance and happiness, but offers opportunities to positively affect those around us.

If the importance of connections is so obvious why do we need reminding? In his new book *American Mania: When More Is Not Enough,* Dr. Peter Whybrow, director of the Semel Institute of Neuroscience and Human Behavior, asserts that Americans are addicted to the pleasure that comes from turbocharged lives. Our "pursuit of more" is driven by pleasure centers in the brain. In this addictive rush, we may end up compromising the one thing that can make us truly happy: our relationships.

Maintaining interpersonal relationships helps us to realize what is important as opposed to what is ephemeral. Relationships provide balance during our growth toward greatness by grounding us in our humanity. So much focus in business and society is placed on process, formula, and machine-like precision that we can forget the wonder of being human — our foibles, flexibility, and resiliency. Even language reflects our disconnectedness. Consider that the new buzzword for women's choice to resume or leave a job is "on-ramping" or "off-ramping." They aren't cars, they're people!

Realizing our interconnectedness is essential in our pursuit of greatness. In a recent study published in *Harvard Business Review,* researcher Marcus Buckingham reveals that great leaders focus on engaging people's hearts to create vision and motivation. Great managers focus on each individual's strengths, and then how to maximize those strengths to benefit both organization *and* individual.

And the same interconnectedness that helps us create balance and happiness, also offers us an opportunity to affect, positively or negatively, everyone we encounter. We know a young couple with an 18-month old daughter they consciously choose to greet every morning with a smile no matter how early she awakens. "Why should she have to wake up to grumpy faces?" they asked. The result so far? A child who rarely cries and wakes up happy and cheerful.

So, people matter. All the bling and status in the world will never satiate our brain's pleasure centers, nor bring us balance as we pursue personal greatness. Remembering interpersonal connectedness can bring balance and happiness while simultaneously affording us the opportunity to positively affect others. There is no such thing as "a man [or woman] of no importance."

Has Greatness Been Watered Down?
April 2005

Earlier this month, at a national conference where we were facilitating a session about greatness, a participant began his comments by quoting, "If everyone is great, then no one is great" from the animated film "The Incredibles." The dialogue that followed challenged some conclusions we've drawn during THE GREATNESS PROJECT.

The discussion revolved around our definition, derived from surveys, that greatness is "living up to our personal value system every day." Participants challenged this from two perspectives. Some argued that the definition itself is a mediocre approximation, aligning "real" greatness with an "I'm okay, you're okay" mentality. Others argued that greatness must be extreme, like a rare action or moment that stands alone and marks a significant moment.

Charles Murray, in the introduction to *Human Accomplishment* writes, "At irregular times and in scattered settings, human beings have achieved great things." He proposes that great achievements have an incredibly powerful, long-lasting, positive effect on the world at large.

We might assume that Murray does not believe everyone can achieve greatness because, in his opinion, so few have. Perhaps an individual can achieve great moments, but that does not mean they are great individuals. (Our topic for the next issue.) Murray argues that there are certain ages and cultures that encouraged greatness and, using the scientific method, he points out that we do not live in one of those cultures.

Greatness, by its nature, seems to raise some individuals and their actions above the rest. And yet, many argue that when we raise up a few individuals as "great" role models, we put down everyone else. Currently, we either create opportunities to acknowledge everyone so that no one is singled out as better or less than, or we offer more support to those who struggle so that we can "level the playing field." Even our overuse of the superlatives "great," "fantastic," "incredible," have reduced their power to the impact of glib advertising copy. We want to address two issues.

First, we have to question the essence of greatness. Does greatness necessarily lead to a hierarchy? Or, is it possible for each individual to achieve personal greatness and simultaneously strive toward societal greatness?

In *Atlas Shrugged*, Ayn Rand imagines a society bent on creating equality by offering support and incentives to those who cannot excel and inhibiting those who do excel. In her version of the world, those who desire greatness eventually retreat to create their own society, leaving the rest to their own destruction.

Secondly, because only we can identify our personal standard for greatness, do we underestimate our ability to achieve greatness by diluting greatness itself? And yet, if we make the standard too high, will that de-motivate us?

In "The Incredibles" all the super-heroes (and heroines) are ordered to live "normal" lives. They become frustrated because society will not allow them the unbridled use of their powers. The rise of a villain intent on eliminating all super-heroes is the only thing that shakes them and society from turpitude and into realizing that their super gifts are necessary and valuable.

Do we delude ourselves by diluting greatness? Can we define greatness in a far-reaching challenging way without losing our willingness to strive for it?

Great Moment or Great Individual?
May 2005

When asked recently about his life, a friend replied, "Moments of brilliance; decades of mediocrity." Although he was being facetious, we were stunned by the accuracy with which he described our own lives. Committing to greatness comes much more easily than sustaining it. Does the consistent achievement of greatness establish us as great? Or, can a select few events, perhaps only one, propel us into the realm of greatness?

We all know individuals who, in one life-changing moment, become great. Rudy Giuliani was simply the mayor of New York City (and not that beloved) when terrorists attacked on September 11. His response and presence became legendary and now he is world-renowned. Rosa Parks was simply on her way home from work and too tired to move to the back of the bus. Her actions sparked the bus boycott that fueled the smoldering civil rights movement of the 1960s. There are many individuals throughout history who seem to have been "in the right place at the right time."

It could be argued that these individuals became great because of a single chance they had. In one select moment, they had an opportunity to do something heroic, patriotic, daring, contradictory, or controversial. Taking that opportunity, they were vaulted by some higher consciousness into greatness and what they did transcended the limitations of time and geography.

Did the specific situation make the individual great? Or, did an already present spark of greatness simply catch fire at the right moment? When we conducted our initial survey, "constancy" emerged as an essential factor defining greatness. Our respondents identified greatness as living up to a personal value system every day; the significance of this was not lost on us.

We realized that most of those we surveyed believed that great individuals nurture the seed of greatness within themselves. Occasionally, they have an opportunity to manifest their personal values and then that moment is vaulted into legend because it happened to be a transformational moment.

We say that individuals do not just turn on their greatness at the right time. These moments do not so much "happen" to great individuals but great individuals, because of who they are, transform these moments. They bring to that precious time values, beliefs, and actions they live every day. What they do and how they do it is as natural to them as breathing. Occasionally, the individual and the transformative moment intersect.

Every day, we're confronted with the reality of life. We can choose to let life victimize us and blame life for what we have not accomplished, or we can strive to live our greatness.

Identifying our values, beliefs, and moral actions, we can live in a conscious awareness that everything we do matters. In striving to live our personal greatness every day, we can be fully present to those we encounter and to every moment. When transformative moments occur or pivotal people arrive in our lives, we don't have to worry about "turning it on." Living our greatness is something we always strive to do.

There really is, then, no "great moment." Occasionally there are transformative moments that elude many of us by their mundane façade. However, the individual who is attempting to live greatness each and every day, scrapes off the patina of the ordinary to transform even the most mundane encounters. It's not the moment that matters as much as individuals who make the ordinary event, extraordinary.

Who Is Your Guru?
June 2005

An ancient Asian proverb advises that "when the student is ready, the teacher will appear." In our studies, a key element of greatness is the willingness to listen to new ideas, to hear concepts that challenge our worldview. Yet, two developmental challenges are contained in the aforementioned proverb. How do we become "ready" to listen and learn, and who is our "teacher?"

Listening is quickly becoming a lost discipline. Most of us have neither the time nor inclination to sit at the feet of anyone and listen to retain some of their wisdom. By adulthood, we have developed mental models of how the world works, how we relate to the world, and what information is vital to us. These mental models, formed as we developed, inhibit us from listening openly because we tend to seek validation for what we already know. We tend to discard new ideas because they do not substantiate our models. Awareness of our own mental models is the first step to a regular discipline of allowing ourselves to be challenged. Only then can we hear a new idea.

Time is also an element that robs us of our ability to listen. We've become a culture that's always on the move and prefers information in "sound bytes" so we can digest them and move on. Davenport and Beck in *The Attention Economy* note that the entire attention span for the average adult is approximately seven minutes. So much for sitting at the feet of any guru! Developing a discipline for exploring a topic deeply can easily enhance our capability of learning new ideas.

As for the "teacher" appearing, our guess is that many "teachers" have passed us by because we did not recognize them. Many of us tend to think of gurus as older, wizened, Yoda-like characters who spout wisdom in fortune cookie phrases.

For example, Melissa looks younger than her 23 years which doesn't offer a lot of comfort when you are flat on your back and she is holding weights over your head. A personal trainer at our local gym, she shatters the mental model that wisdom comes with age because though she is paid to enhance the body, she does so by challenging the mind.

Melissa could easily be dismissed as "just a young, inexperienced trainer" until you observe her. Unlike most personal trainers, she does not tell you the number of repetitions you need to do and then count them out. She watches your body and breathing and lets you know when it's time to stop.

By listening to and observing her, we learned that it's not what the trainer wants to impose that's important, but what the student is capable of learning. That wisdom profoundly affects how we conduct our coaching of others and yet it would have been so easily missed if we just dismissed Melissa because of her youth and seeming inexperience and not accepted her as a teacher.

Life provides a plethora of teachers and teachable moments. Sometimes reality stares us in the face with a profound message and we just pass by hurrying to our next meeting. Books offer us the possibilities of new thoughts, ideas, and worlds, but too often we cannot take time to appreciate their content. Even nature provides the possibility of illumination, if only we realize the wisdom pronounced from dawn to dusk.

Our personal greatness is enhanced by listening to the collective wisdom that surrounds us and acknowledging the teacher who offers that wisdom. Who is your guru?

Are We Primed for Greatness?
July 2005

With whom do we surround ourselves? Do the people around us offer vocal encouragement? The power of what they say to us has more impact on our success or failure than any of us may realize.

Whenever you sit next to someone complaining about life, about work, and about everything else, do you sense that you're losing energy? Do you start feeling depressed? If so, you are not alone. The other person's griping affects us on a subconscious level and for a period of time afterward, we will be more critical and less accepting of the challenges that confront us. The words we hear have a direct, powerful, and immediate impact on our reactions and behaviors.

John Bargh, a psychologist affiliated with New York University, conducted a series of what he terms "priming experiments." He wanted to determine how much impact words have on human behavior. In one experiment, subjects were asked to take a series of scrambled words and put them into sentences. Within the scramble were words directly related to aging. Bargh discovered that research subjects walked more slowly and gingerly out of the room than when they arrived, apparently affected subconsciously by words within the test.

A second experiment proved even more revealing. Two groups of subjects were asked to complete a scramble test in which one group worked with words specifically related to aggression, while the other group unscrambled sentences with words relating to patience.

The tests lasted five minutes after which the subjects were asked to walk down the hall and talk to one of the test administrators. Bargh set up the scene so that the administrator would be engaged in a 10 minute conversation. He wanted to see if after being "primed" differently how long it would take subjects in either group to interrupt.

The group that was primed for aggression tolerated five minutes before interrupting the conversation. What amazed Bargh was that 82% of subjects in the second group never interrupted at all. If the experiment hadn't ended after 10 minutes, some of the "patient" subject group might have continued to wait.

The effects of priming aren't trivial; they begin early in our development as we learn what to think about boys and girls, men and women, different races and ethnicities and, most importantly, what we think about ourselves. Professor Bargh's experiments help us to realize that priming continues throughout our life.

Can people be primed for greatness? With enough positive words and images can success be assisted?

Two Dutch researchers worked with positive and negative imagery to assess its effect on tests. One subject group was asked to think for five minutes about what it would mean to be a professor and then write down what came to mind. A second group was asked to think about what it would mean to be a criminal and then write it down. Next, both groups took the same 42 question test. The "professor" group correctly answered 52.6% of the questions; the "criminal" group answered 42.6% correctly. The first group was primed to be in a "smart" frame of mind.

Every time we hear feedback, we process it consciously and subconsciously. This feedback and our awareness of ourselves has a powerful impact on our performance. To whom do we listen? Who encourages us? Are we priming ourselves — and others — to achieve greatness?

Reflection Time
August 2005

For many, summer offers an opportunity to slow down, even vacation if we have a chance. Slowing down provides time for reflection. We offer these following questions for your own reflection. If you are willing, please send your reflections to us for our ongoing research on greatness. Of course, we will not use your name without permission and we will continue to publish findings in our monthly newsletters. Thank you! We hope you enjoy this opportunity for reflection — and the rest of your summer.

Questions for reflection:

- In what ways are you either closer to or further away from living your personal greatness? What might be in the way of your greatness goals?
- What changes in your life would you need to make to get closer to living your personal greatness?
- Who are the people around you (if any) who motivate you the most?
- Have you told them what they mean to you?
- What inspires you to continue your pursuit of personal greatness?
- Does spirituality or religion affect your pursuit of greatness? If so, how?
- How does the way you strive to live personal greatness affect those around you?

Room to Zoom
September 2005

Melissa doesn't count repetitions. Quietly, she watches her clients work out and determines how many more repetitions can be done. Just when clients believe they are at their last repetition, she asks them to do more and, almost miraculously, they can. Melissa is a personal trainer who believes that most of us create low expectations of our abilities. Her job is to help others exceed their expectations. She does that and with her encouragement, people often exceed even her high expectations.

Most research indicates that setting goals is a key part of achieving greatness. This is essentially correct. However, we've found that there's a tendency for many of us to unconsciously set relatively attainable goals; not really stretching ourselves. Whether this is from a conscious effort to ensure success, or from a fear of failure, short-sightedness ultimately limits our ability to develop in a life-changing way. Essentially, we sell ourselves short. We are capable of more.

Why do some individuals see the stars when the rest of us see a ceiling? Some people set high goals thanks to the profound belief and guidance of someone else, or an innate ability to set aside the desire to remain safe. They willingly, or with guidance, seek a challenge that seems too great to attain.

Melissa is a perfect example of someone who, through training and instinct, knows that people can be pushed further. They can do more than they realize. Some of us need these people in our lives. Whether parents, teachers, coaches, friends or mentors, these individuals see possibilities for us that we cannot. They challenge us to focus on the stars. Their vision allows us to move beyond mediocrity and into the realm of personal greatness.

Some individuals, without guidance, will challenge themselves to do more, even when it appears they have already attained greatness. Steve Jobs, the founder of Apple, was CEO of one of the most successful enterprises in the country, voted out of office by the board, and then brought back in as CEO. Amazingly, Jobs showed no fear as he led Apple back into the forefront of technology through music. We might think that he has earned the right to relax, yet last year he told a group of Apple executives, "Playing it safe is the most dangerous thing we can do. We have to get bolder."

Many of us are afraid to set our goals too high. We worry about getting frustrated with ourselves in our attempts to reach the unreachable. And yet, lower goals will eventually frustrate us because we know we can do more. Balance comes from setting high goals while enjoying our attempts to attain them. We can find comfort in realizing that our grand attempt will help us to achieve significant goals.

Whether through coaching or innate drive, striving for greatness demands that we constantly set challenging goals. Safety gained through inertia gradually erects a ceiling that may indeed provide security, but will prevent us from moving further. Only when we create room to zoom, can we hope to fulfill personal greatness.

What do you think?

Do You Display Neotony?
October 2005

This past week, we had the opportunity to watch a rising corporate leader speak about his business to a group of high-potential employees. As he strode to the front of the group to promote his ideas, he smiled broadly, gestured effusively, and could barely contain the excitement in his voice.

The audience was captivated by his content, but mostly by his style; they couldn't take their eyes off him. A voice behind us said, "He's just like a little kid with a new toy." They were absolutely right. The power of his message was enhanced by his excitement and wonder over all the possibilities. These child-like characteristics engaged us and drew us to him. This is one of the qualities we see in great individuals: a childlike wonder, awe, and enthusiasm for the world.

Many of us, as we grew up, were told, "Act your age." Essentially, this meant behaving older than our chronological age, or to be "mature." But all too often, maturity meant shutting down the excitement of engaging with our world.

We still hear excited children being told to use "their inside voice" when they get too loud. Once in the school system, children learn quickly to quench enthusiasm for new ideas out of fear about what other kids will say.

When we land our first job, we steel ourselves to look mature and serious so that we will fit in with other employees. We construct a society that represses our joy and enthusiasm for life or work because exuberance seems immature or irrelevant.

Yet when we meet individuals who still have a zest for life, especially in later years, or a passionate love for what they do, we are drawn to them. Borrowing a concept from zoology, this is called neotony, or the retention of youthful characteristics in adulthood. Warren Bennis in his book, *Geeks and Geezers,* used this concept to describe both new and established leaders and to explain why they are so compelling.

Bennis calls neotony an appropriate metaphor for adults who, through their passion for life, influence others powerfully. These individuals are still capable of wonder and awe. They wake up each day eager to learn, live, and grow. These qualities are still present well into their mature years.

Why are these characteristics so engaging? Why are we drawn to individuals who have them? Too often many of us just seem tired. Whether working, ferrying children to and from activities, or even relaxing, most adults seem to exude exhaustion. We are drawn to those who have energy and excitement. We want to understand what they're experiencing, although sometimes we don't believe they're for real and await the façade's eventual collapse into ruin.

Reengaging your passion — what you love about life — is exhilarating. If you can uncover what you love about your work, you become inspired to create, produce, and perform at a much higher level. It's no longer "work." Just think about how your life would be transformed if you chose to encounter your world with childlike awe and wonder.

When the executive at the conference finished speaking, he was radiant. He was not tired, but energized by sharing his ideas with the group. The group, in turn, was energized by him. What unleashes your wonder, awe, and excitement? What do you love? How can you regain that lost love?

Trash Talk

November 2005

"Bad news is good news" is a well-worn adage in the newspaper business because bad news sells papers. Perhaps this explains the current proliferation of gossip sheets and magazines that pillory leaders, actors, and athletes with abandon and yet, if confronted with the truth, bury the retraction. We seem to be a nation that loves gossip and it follows us into our communities, our workplaces, and even our families. Does this insistence on finding and shattering the clay feet of successful individuals help create an environment of greatness? Not in the slightest.

Perhaps gossip grows out of envy or a desire to level the playing field. And while it may bring an exceptional person down, it never elevates anyone involved. Proponents righteously proclaim that they seek the truth, yet the truth never seems balanced with positive accomplishments. If there's some dark deed in someone's past for which they have atoned, how is being reminded about it helpful? Does knowing this make us better people?

Gossip and scandal, even when true, serve no one and perversely multiplies and distorts as it's shared. Realizing how pernicious gossip can be might make us pause, but there is almost no way to assess the damage. Perhaps an old Italian story might help.

A man went to confession and confessed that he had gossiped about a leader in the city. The priest listened sagely and then suggested his penance. "Take a bag full of feathers and go to the highest tower in the city. Release the bag of feathers and then come back to see me." The man did as he was told and then returned to the priest. The priest said to him, "Your penance is to go and collect all the feathers you released." Shocked, the man complained, "Father, that would be impossible. I would have no idea where all of the feathers went, they could have gone anywhere." "Exactly," the priest replied, "and so your gossip will spread throughout the city and go to all corners and you will never know where your malicious talk has spread." The man went away vowing never to gossip again.

Perhaps there's a way to redirect the talkative nature of humans. We've already explored the power of positive words in other articles, both as specific feedback and as internal dialogue. Consider this: How would your work, community, or home environment change if you spoke about others in only positive terms? Instead of sharing "clay-feet-shattering" information about someone, what if you shared only that person's good ideas and actions? What if you committed to building people up instead of verbally tearing them down? What if you encouraged others to greater things by listening to positive stories? Now *that* would be an environment of greatness.

We play a role in creating our environment. Everyone has a time in life when she or he stumbled, made the wrong choice, or failed to help someone. We can elect to find those faults, to somehow believe that we're righteous or perfect enough to enlighten others about imperfections we see. Or, we can create environments that assist every person to thrive, realizing essentially that to be fully human means being capable of great errors as well as great deeds.

Great environments focus on great deeds. Previous challenges are used as inspiration for future possibilities. Great environments honor the reality of being human and celebrate the greatness of which we are all capable. What are you doing to create a great environment?

True Grit
December 2005

The expression, "Quitters never win and winners never quit," is placed firmly in the minds of many children to teach them perseverance. Contrasted against innate talent or intelligence, touting perseverance seems like a vague attempt to soothe bruised egos. Yet, new research points to the power of persistence and tenacity in achieving greatness. Additionally grit, it seems, can be cultivated and strengthened.

We sometimes acknowledge others who are more successful by suggesting that they are "more intelligent," "more talented," or "lucky." We might even take comfort in the supposedly immutable truth that they were born to succeed and we were not. However, studies by Dr. Robert Sternberg (Tufts University) and Dr. Martin Seligman (University of Pennsylvania) suggest that only 25% of successful job performance can be attributed to IQ, the rest of the factors are more ambiguous.

As recently reported in *Psychology Today*, new studies at the University of Pennsylvania uncover the power of grit in achieving success at school, work, and other pursuits.

Grit is defined as "the determination to accomplish an ambitious, long-term goal despite the inevitable obstacles." These studies seek to understand the true nature of grit and how to develop it in children and adults. What's certain is that developing and nurturing grit has value to everyone.

The article suggests seven ways to nurture grit in others. We believe these may also be applied to achieving personal greatness.

HELP PEOPLE FIND THEIR PASSION

When you're passionate about what you're doing, you are more likely to persevere when things get difficult. *What is your passion?*

DON'T WORRY ABOUT BALANCE

No one can be great at everything. Identify what you do well and focus on it. *What are you good at?*

PROVIDE CRITICISM LESSONS

Learning how to receive criticism without losing motivation will help prevent derailment when striving to complete a task or achieve a goal. *Can you hear criticism dispassionately?*

BE A MODEL OF GRITTINESS

People imitate what they see. Model grittiness for others and identify a role model for yourself. *Who is your "grittiness" role model?*

OFFER CHALLENGES

Offer challenges or take on challenges that require sustained effort, but aren't impossible to attain. *What is your next challenge?*

TEACH PEOPLE HOW TO HANDLE AND LEARN FROM FAILURE

Developing coping mechanisms is essential because there are always setbacks and failures on the way to achievement. *What are your coping mechanisms?*

ENCOURAGE OPTIMISM

Having a positive sense of the future is directly linked to perseverance. *Are you optimistic about the future?*

Nurturing grit may seem counter-cultural in a society like ours that's so focused on instant gratification. Yet, if success can be attained more readily by fostering grit, we say that developing true grit in ourselves and others is worth the effort.

What Time Is It?

January 2006

Is this scene familiar? Family or friends gather to eat at home or a restaurant. A phone rings. Someone answers the phone and is swept up in a conversation that doesn't concern or involve anyone else present.

Another scenario: during conversations with families, friends, or business colleagues you become uncomfortably but acutely aware that the other person is not paying attention to you; either they are text messaging a friend, dialing or answering their cell phone, or staring at you with the glazed look of someone lost in space.

Welcome to 2006. We have, it seems, created a society where everyone is rushed, preoccupied, or somewhere else. To attain personal greatness, we need to be aware of this growing societal epidemic and master the discipline to combat it.

What is this societal epidemic? Instant, 24/7 information offers us all we need to know about what others are doing. Yet it's not information that challenges us but instead the subtle, insidious belief that real life is happening everywhere else, rather than right where we are.

The epidemic we suffer from is **F.M.S.**: 'fraid of **m**issing **s**omething. It's manifested in our constant need to know what others are doing, to rush what is occurring right now and move on to something else (supposedly better), or to attempt to do many things simultaneously so we won't miss out on anything. How do we combat this epidemic?

Patrick McDonnell is not a philosopher by profession, he is a cartoonist. Drawing the comic strip "Mutts," Patrick offers tidbits of wisdom through the lives and voices of a small family and their dog and cat. In a recent Sunday strip, the dog asks the cat a question. "Hey, Mooch, do you know what time it is?" "Sure," replies Mooch. "It's NOW. It's always now. Here … look at my watch." And Mooch shows his watch which only has one hand pointing to the word "Now" and adds, "It's never wrong." That concept of time is a discipline many of us would do well to learn.

Changing behavior begins by becoming aware of current behavior. Notice how often you are not in the moment. Do you find yourself focusing on other tasks while in the middle of one that's not yet complete? Are you trying to recall what someone just said because you weren't really listening? When you contact friends, does it always seem they're having a better time than you?

Once aware of how you have been caught up in the F.M.S. epidemic, the second step is clearing the way for new behavior. Simply slowing down or stopping the influx of extraneous information will eliminate some of the distractions. Turning off your cell phone, at least while visiting with friends and family, communicates a powerful message about how important they are. Focusing on your conversation with someone elevates their sense of self worth and offers the chance to learn more about them.

Finally, how about accepting that the only time we ever have is right now. This means making whatever you are doing or whomever you are with preeminent. Great individuals have a remarkable ability to focus on the task or person in front of them. This discipline can transform your world; every moment becomes an opportunity to discover the joy of work, the richness of connection with others, or even the peace of relaxation. Eckhart Tolle suggests simply, "Always say 'yes' to the present moment."

What time is it? It's always **NOW**.

The Energizers
February 2006

When Monday morning arrives, do you feel energized by the prospect of tackling fulfilling work? Or does the week's tasks seem so daunting and draining you'd rather return to bed? What energizes you to strive toward achievement? In *Human Accomplishment* (Harper Collins, 2003), Charles Murray identifies individual and cultural sources that energize human accomplishment.

First, Murray acknowledges that excellence requires hard work. "Fame can come easily and overnight, but excellence is almost always accompanied by a crushing workload, pursued with single-minded intensity." Few people achieve excellence or greatness without working extraordinarily hard, although most who are passionate about a goal don't view what they do as hard work. Time and effort simply fly by as they engage in this drive to achieve. Still, this drive requires an enormous amount of energy. Energy needs fuel.

Murray points out that *purpose* is a significant source of energy. From studying great individuals and great achievements, Murray suggests that, "the willingness to engage in such monomaniacal levels of effort... is related to a sense of vocation." (He hedges on the common definition of vocation as being "called by God," offering a more generalized definition that focuses awareness of one's life mission; their purpose.)

What we do with this sense of purpose is a great source of energy. Your challenge lies in becoming aware of your purpose and then remembering it so you feel renewed and refreshed on a daily basis.

Next, Murray suggests that *autonomy* is another significant source of energy. For him, "a major stream of human accomplishment is fostered by a culture that encourages the belief that individuals can act efficaciously as individuals, and enables them to do so." For individuals, autonomy is defined as the belief in one's individual power to fulfill life purpose through action. This concept does not preclude individuals from working together, but emphasizes the point that creativity may ultimately come down to small solitary acts.

Much of the energy derived from autonomy stems from an awareness that life purpose can be pursued despite obstacles, disagreement, peer pressure, or confrontation. The more an individual *willingly* stands alone to achieve a goal, the greater the energy that person will generate. And if the surrounding culture supports autonomy, creativity and achievement will be all the greater.

Our research indicates that many people can identify some purpose in life, whether a long-term goal, or a temporary one. Most of us, however, are challenged by our lack of autonomy. Whether we're unwilling to challenge a culture, stand up for a new idea, resist the urge to give in to pressure from others, we short change ourselves by dodging the countercultural possibilities that creativity and achievement demand. Autonomy requires realizing that pursuing our goals may take us out of the mainstream.

Are you willing to accept the realities of true autonomy and thus energize your pursuit of greatness?

A Great Fit
March 2006

If you've ever struggled to assemble something that came with "simple, easy-to-read instructions," you understand the frustration of stripping the wrong bolt only to discover (later) the correct one that fit beautifully into place. That image relates perfectly to achieving greatness; there has to be the right fit.

Think about how strongly you agree with the following statement: "At work (at home, or in my life) I get to do what I do best every day." The Gallup organization, which posed this question to more than two million people over the past few years, discovered it was the most important question they asked. How respondents answered revealed a direct link to their productivity and performance. Respondents who agreed emphatically with the statement and felt that they got to do what they did best each day, also reported performance that was significantly higher than those who could not agree with the statement.

We found this research to be particularly noteworthy for our purposes. Can individuals unleash their own greatness in an environment that does not play to their strengths? Can individuals who are great at one area, also be great in another? The simple answer is "no." Great individuals either find an environment that plays to their strengths or they create them. They rarely achieve greatness in environments that exploit their weaknesses.

We have never discussed "fit" in the context of THE GREATNESS PROJECT, but this research opened our eyes. To completely unleash greatness, individuals need to first understand their unique talents and gifts, and then they need to find or create the best environment that will allow their full expression.

Understanding our own unique talents presents the first challenge. This is not about being simply good at something; we have to look beyond competence. Analyzing where we have a natural strength or ability is only the beginning of the process. Think about (and write down) everything that comes easily and naturally. Perhaps writing, speaking, or creating art is so natural we don't have to think about it. Our talent could also be in the way we relate to people, or even in the way we think.

Once we've identified our natural talents, then we need to identify where they fit best. Begin by drilling deeper into how and where that talent is best utilized. For example, if you have a talent for strategic thinking and are able to easily think through the course of action and the repercussions of various projects, you are best positioned where you can use that talent every day if possible. Finding yourself in a position that allows only time-honored ideas will bore you at best or continually frustrate you. The problem in that position is you're not playing to your talent. We have two choices if we're already in a position that doesn't play to our talents. Either we need to discover how to tap into our talents wherever we are, or look for a more suitable position.

Discovering the right fit takes thoughtful awareness of our capabilities and understanding how we can best play to our strengths. And yet, fit is not something we can just hope to have. We must develop a strategy to either find a place where we can excel, or create that place for ourselves.

Playing with Plato
April 2006

Discussions about and attempts to achieve greatness often falter because of conflicting concepts about the essence of greatness. Understanding and measuring greatness requires a common language for key concepts. We suggest revisiting Plato, who introduced three concepts for judging something's worth: the true, the beautiful, and the good. Applying these criteria can help us discover new ways of achieving personal greatness.

Current concepts about greatness focus either on accomplishment or fame. As a result, instead of gaining deeper insight into human possibility, we're often left feeling demoralized because we have not done enough, don't have enough, or aren't well known enough. Knowing that fame, glamour, and power will fade, it makes sense to turn our attention to what is true, beautiful, and good. "Conceptions of the good, true, and beautiful prevailing at any given time concretely affect how excellence manifests itself." (Charles Murray, Human Accomplishment)

Both Plato and Aristotle defined the "good" as excellence in human-ness. Their concept embraced the greatest and finest aspects of what it means to be human (e.g., heroism, selflessness, creativity, joy). Employing this concept shifts the focus of greatness to an appreciation for internal development, i.e. how do I become a better woman or man?

How would you define the "good" (excellence in human-ness) in your life? What does/would it look like? What are you doing to achieve it?

Identifying the "true" is equally challenging. We all know the concept, even if we disagree on its exact definition. For example, if we place all our daily news sources under the microscope of "truth," it pierces the ambiguous nature of politics, sensationalism, innuendo, etc. and illuminates the tainted reality of much that we hear or read. In the same way, applying the "true" as we strive to achieve greatness should shift our focus to becoming more aware of whether and how true we are to ourselves, rather than what is fleeting. (For some of us this may require making time to discover who we are.)

What does the "true" look like in your life? How can you become more authentic in all that you say and do?

Finally, shifting our awareness to the beauty of things, simply as they are, challenges our current notions of the "beautiful." Is there anything more beautiful than something being what it was created to be?

Can you identify the "beautiful" in you? How can you bring joy to everything you do every day?

Truth. Beauty. Goodness. These three concepts can shift our focus — and our actions — from exaggerated forms of societal excess to deeper and more universal truths. Embracing them invites us into self-examination and draws us closer to personal greatness.

How Do You Define Success?
May 2006

"Success needs to be redefined. This is because if you read the definition of success in the dictionary, it sounds like it was written for sociopaths." With this *bon mot*, Stewart Emery, co-author on a soon to be published book about successful individuals, challenges more than Webster. He tosses down the gauntlet to our society and challenges us to redefine for ourselves what success means.

Since beginning our study of greatness in August 2001, we find ourselves continually uncovering societal concepts of success and greatness that impede the individual's ability to move toward personal greatness. Sometimes subtle, often overt, these concepts seduce people into believing that monetary gain or tangible assets are either the means to the end, or are an end themselves. They lead people away from internal development or outward connection to the larger community. Many of us have internalized these ideas without realizing we've done so. As a result, we often feel conflicted between higher values and the societal demands that we define ourselves by what we have. Perhaps it's time to define what we seek.

Mark Thompson and Stewart Emery, who have researched successful individuals for the past 10 years, will soon release their findings in the book, *Success Built to Last*. In an interview with Knowledge@Wharton they challenged dictionary definitions of success because, as Emery notes, "If you go to Oxford or Webster — whether you take a dictionary from either side of the Atlantic — they define success in the same way, as the accumulation of influence, power, wealth and accolades. We see a lot of people chasing that kind of success."

What Thompson and Emery discovered resonates with what we've learned while studying greatness. Emery put it this way, "A lot of people are experiencing incredible success. Although they don't think about it per se, they have rich lives and they are having an impact that will probably benefit the world way beyond their lifetime. The traditional definition of success doesn't fit their lives at all."

By understanding what we really think success means and perhaps redefining it, we can move toward our own personal greatness. We, however, are not challenging Webster and Oxford. Instead, we offer this as a personal challenge for you. Does the definition of success fit your personal belief system? If it doesn't, you might consider redefining it for yourself!

Emery and Thompson offer their idea of success, not in a definition but in three fundamental principles that their interviewees suggested lead to success. According to Thompson, these three do not stand alone, but interact with and play off each other: meaning, thought, and action. Thompson offers this clarification, "We found that individuals across the spectrum of professions were striving to find something that mattered to them in a very fundamental way. This prompted them to drive their thoughts to frame a way of producing those results and then acting on those results."

If what we think drives what we do, how do you define success?

Different Values
June 2006

Is a societal shift revealing a major change in how we value ourselves and each other?

There seems to be a growing trend in the US to work either part or full time during retirement. This is being driven by a number of factors, not least of which is the fact that many reach retirement without the necessary savings. They are "forced" to do work to supplement their income or to provide medical benefits. Others continue working because it offers them a purpose. We think something else more insidious may be involved: the notion that simply relaxation is unacceptable. This philosophical shift cuts directly to what we consider of value. It deserves our careful consideration.

Last week, we were invited to a retirement party for a friend who is a senior executive at a global company. A day later he called to chat and we had the opportunity to congratulate him. We asked what he was going to do during retirement. "Nothing," he said. We questioned his wisdom, suggesting that he might want to either continue working or become involved in a philanthropic endeavor. His reply was eye-opening. "I've been preparing for this moment since I was 18 years old," he said. "I just want to relax and enjoy life."

After the phone call ended, we talked about how we had been seduced into the idea that people had to do something in retirement. More serious was how we were reinforcing the underlying notion that it is simply unacceptable to do nothing; there's only value in doing.

Many of us grew up being told that "idle hands are the devil's workshop." Being busy would give us no time to get into trouble. As we listen currently to parents and kids talk about their crazy schedules, we observe how this dictum has been taken to a whole new level. Children no longer spend long, lazy summer afternoons as their imagination and spontaneity dictate. Today's children are so completely scheduled, they have little or no relaxation time. Adults tend to create even more restricting schedules for themselves. Overcommitment and exhaustion are the norm for everyone.

There is a growing belief that we are what we do or what we produce; that the value of being human is only in what we give back to society or what we have gathered for ourselves.

Notice how often many of us describe who we are relative to what we do. We describe ourselves as homemakers, managers, consultants, authors, accountants, and the like. When asked, "How are you doing?" we often reply with a litany of what we've accomplished as though someone was keeping track. The benefit of this belief system is that people are encouraged to be functioning members of society, giving back in whatever way they can. Yet it also challenges how we value our life. Are we still valuable if we cannot (or choose not to) produce?

There are those who believe differently about their value and the value of others. They believe that each human being is a treasure and that life becomes more precious by taking time to reflect on it. They remain unconvinced that production and ownership define success. Rather, they create their work around their life, leaving time to enjoy moments and people.

These two different notions of human value confront us each day. Which one do you choose to live?

Where Is the Spotlight?

July 2006

"Me, me, me, it's all about me. What about you? What do you think about me?" This Bette Midler line from the movie "Beaches," epitomizes the self-aggrandizing nature of many in our society. They seek the spotlight and are reluctant to share it. Their conversational style is a near-zero tolerance stance for dialogue. They wait for people to stop talking or blatantly interrupt to foist their opinions or thoughts on others. This trend is so prevalent that it is the focus of Charles Derber's book, *The Pursuit of Attention*. Seem familiar?

Listening is a dying art; being present seems impossible; balanced conversation is a goal few strive to attain. Are great people as guilty of this desperate ego-stroking as the rest of us?

G.K. Chesterton once said, "The truly great person is the one who makes every person feel great." With all due respect to Mr. Chesterton, contemporary society elevates and holds up as models of greatness those who have offered incredible advances. But these same individuals may not be able to talk about anything but themselves and their work. However, all is not lost. Notwithstanding our society's demand for instant communication with everyone else-where, some individuals set themselves apart by their amazing ability to focus on the person right in front of them.

What does this focus do for the other person? At a conference in California, a participant told us a story that illustrates the point perfectly. "In Queen Victoria's time, a young woman had the good fortune of being escorted to dinner by William E. Gladstone, who was considered one of the most brilliant statesmen of the 19th century.

On the following evening, the same young lady was escorted by Benjamin Disraeli, novelist, statesman, and twice prime minister of Great Britain. When asked for her impression of these two great rivals, she replied, 'After an evening with Gladstone, I thought he was the most brilliant man I'd ever met. After an evening with Disraeli, I thought myself to be the most fascinating woman in the world!'"

Allowing the other person to be the focus of attention requires ego strength; it also requires an ability to listen to, focus on, and value the other person. Seems like too much work? Not once you begin practicing.

Ego strength allows the spotlight to shine on the other without needing to steal it back. This quality permits the other to enjoy their moment without competing for attention. Communication involves asking questions rather than making statements. It is about knowing what to ask and when. In this context, listening is not simply being quiet; it involves the active pursuit of knowledge about the other. Focus is manifested through direct eye contact and not the flitting, furtive glancing around for someone more important. Focus can be the key to making someone feel they are truly valued.

Our studies reveal that individuals who seek greatness realize they have the power to make choices that determine who they are and what they can accomplish. Allowing others to be the center of attention, feel listened to and valued is one such choice. We can decide how others will experience time with us. Will they walk away believing that we are great, or will they walk away believing that, at least in our eyes, they are? The choice is ours.

Can We Talk?

August 2006

Our society seems to be losing its ability to communicate well. We came to this conclusion after offering a series focused on communication. We conducted informal surveys to ascertain the comfort and confidence professionals have about their ability to communicate. While we applaud their candor, we have to report that the situation does not look good. We examined communications skills in the areas of negotiating, resolving conflict, networking, persuasion, and even making small talk. Many professionals admitted woeful ignorance of even the most basic skills in these domains. Almost all made technology the scapegoat or sacrificial offering.

Why is communication so important? Achieving greatness often depends on the ability of an individual or group to communicate an idea. Whether in an informal setting or a formal presentation, the ability to convey ideas is paramount to success in almost every arena. Unlike many characteristics of greatness that trigger arguments about whether they're innate, communication can be learned. Anyone can master communication skills to project meaning and confidence. Here are four disciplines that, if adopted, will lead to great communication.

Honor words. Words have tremendous power. Placed together strategically, they can change the course of history. Within the flow of any conversation, argument or speech, they convey the speaker's intelligence and intent. How often do you carefully choose words to carry your message? What practice would help you regularly explore new word choices and phraseology?

Craft clear messages. Building a broader context of understanding helps listeners grasp the full meaning of our words. Messages may be effectively crafted around analogy or story. All of us are story tellers, even if we don't realize it. How well do you use stories or analogies to deliver your messages? How often are you aware of stories happening around you that could bring greater meaning to your communications?

Deliver passion. Passion or what we call "zeal" is perhaps the most powerful communication discipline. Messages are easier to believe when the speaker is passionate about the subject. For too many, zeal exited work (and possibly life) years ago. Communication has become tepid at best. What excites and invigorates your communication? Where in your life are you living with joy and enthusiasm? How can you use this to electrify your communication?

Make your word honorable. Great individuals live up to their word. Knowing the power of words, they say what they mean. Yes is yes; no is no. Because we live in a world of nuance, where deals are often secured more by what is not said than what is said, it would seem only natural to forgive the slight lies or misstatements that accompany communication in 2006. However, integrity is a key characteristic of great individuals. Do you keep your word? When and why do you allow yourself to sacrifice honesty for harmony?

We are creatures who communicate constantly by every means available. Great communicators hone their skills through hard work and practice. Words matter. Developing disciplines to enrich communication will immediately affect our work and life, assisting us as we strive for personal greatness.

Are We Conserving Our Compassion?
September 2006

A hurricane wipes out a city and a year later rebuilding is still slow. Poverty abounds and the victims are blamed as though it's their fault. Tragedy happens on a local or national scale and by the next day, it's old news. What has happened to compassion? Have we become too overwhelmed with pain, suffering, and death? A natural survival instinct when one is overwhelmed is to become numb: to withhold compassion. Yet, compassion has always been one of the most powerful characteristics of great individuals; it needs renewal now.

Perhaps withholding compassion should be called the "CNN Syndrome" because of the role that news organization has played in making war, famine, terror, etc. available 24/7. Reality is thrust at us every time we turn on the TV, turn on the radio, or even turn the corner. At a certain point we become overwhelmed and can't take it anymore. And that is when we turn off our desire to help anyone else; we protect ourselves and conserve our compassion.

David Friend, in his new book, **Watching the World Change**, offers readers a startling photograph by Thomas Hoepker. The shot captures a group of friends on a break, chatting away on the Brooklyn waterfront on September 11th, while across the water smoke and residue roll through lower Manhattan. Hoepker, commented to Friend, "They were totally relaxed like any normal afternoon. It's possible they lost people and cared but they were not stirred by it."

So, too, when hurricane Katrina ripped through New Orleans and revealed the raw wound of poverty in the US, we were stirred —

for a moment. We did not seem to linger and ask the difficult questions. We did not wonder why, with all the wealth in this country, we lead the world with the greatest percentage (21%) of children in poverty.

Great individuals do not withhold or conserve their compassion, they give it freely, "spending it" on people, causes and issues that affect them and others. John F. Kennedy put it very well in his well worn statement, "Ask not what your country can do for you. Ask, rather, what you can do for your country." Great individuals know that the willingness to look outside of oneself is essential to compassion.

Looking outside of our self, we cannot remain numb because compassion itself begins with feeling the pain of others. The Latin root of the word "compassion" means literally "to suffer with" and once we permit ourselves to feel again, we will realize that we have plenty of compassion to offer.

And because we might fear being overwhelmed, it's important that we mindfully resume the practice of spending our compassion. Mother Teresa of Calcutta summed up how to spend compassion in two quotes.

"In this life we cannot do great things. We can only do small things with great love."
"I want you to be concerned about your next door neighbor. Do you know your next door neighbor?"

Spending our compassion freely assists those around us. Spending our compassion generously transforms us.

Putting on the Ritz

October 2006

The name, Ritz, connotes luxury, grandeur, and elegance. Through movies, descriptions, and language it has become a common way to describe the uncommon, the elite, the best. As the brand behind the description, the Ritz-Carlton could rest on its laurels, but our recent experience impresses us that, though number one in the world in luxury hotels, Ritz Carlton is not resting. Their focus and signature style offers a great example to both individuals and corporations.

Recently, courtesy of a speaking engagement, we had the opportunity to enjoy the Ritz-Carlton on Amelia Island, Florida. Previous engagements had allowed us to experience the service at other Ritz-Carltons, so we looked forward to our visit. While we enjoyed the exemplary attentions of the staff and the beauty of the venue, we noticed that this experience was different. Notably the signature response, "It would be my pleasure," was missing. However, rather than this marking a decline in their incredible service, it only seemed to enhance it.

Every staff member at this particular Ritz seemed attentive to our every need before we spoke it. We were greeted warmly and once they knew our names, employees were quick to use them and tell them to the next staff member we would encounter. What was different this time was the attentiveness with which our emotional needs were assessed. When a facial and body scrub were interrupted by the fire alarm both were given free because "the experience was interrupted." Choosing to relax at day's end in the bar, we chose a single malt scotch to taste; however when our hostess found that they had none left, she offered us any other scotch on the menu free of charge and suggested we take this opportunity to try a more expensive one.

We watched another guest leave a table because of a bee sting, returning to have the server offer the comfort of tea and toast. Another host observed a guest skipping the meat at a buffet line and after acknowledging this, mentioning there would be salmon at the next buffet, and would that be alright? We had to acknowledge that the "ladies and gentlemen" (as the staff at the Ritz-Carlton are called) were connecting on a much deeper level than just excellent service.

Our perceptions were validated in a recent Gallup Management Journal interview with Simon Cooper, Chief Operating Officer and President of The Ritz-Carlton Hotel Company, L.L.C. Cooper who offered that "we're focusing on the emotional connection between our ladies and gentlemen and our guests." The Ritz-Carlton has become aware, as Cooper states that, "Obviously, guests can't buy things like smiles or relationships or caring service....That's the value proposition — that's how you engage a customer. You engage them emotionally by giving them things they just can't buy anywhere else."

This focus on emotional connection is a move from "client service" toward what we are calling "client hospitality." We "service" machines; connoting a process that is methodical, uniform and not personal. However "hospitality" encompasses the next, very important step of connecting by attending to the personal, emotional level of clients or guests. This is where the best companies are focusing their efforts now so that everyone has an "experience" that binds them to that company.

We can learn from the Ritz as we pursue greatness. Increasingly our culture has become a "me-mine" society with the desire for the spotlight to be directed on us. As early as 1983, Charles Derber, author of The Pursuit of Attention, noted our societal tendency toward self-absorption. In the second edition (published in 2000) he added observations about our societal propensity toward "ego-surfing" (looking for one's name on the internet) as additional evidence of our self-focus.

What makes the Ritz-Carlton great is not their focus on properties, people, or their organization; it's their unrelenting focus on the ladies and gentlemen they serve. Essentially, by their interaction, their emotional connection, and their hospitality, they elevate anyone who walks into their hotels. We feel better by being in their presence, thus creating the Pygmalion Effect (we are treated as great and therefore we perform more to our greatness).

If, in making their motto our own, we would treat others as great individuals and focus on making an emotional connection with them, we could unleash the greatness in everyone we meet and simultaneously unleash our own. Imagine: "We are ladies and gentlemen serving ladies and gentlemen."

Practice Doesn't Make Perfect
November 2006

Fortune magazine believes it has discovered the secret to greatness. The November issue of *Fortune* focuses almost entirely on excellence and their key article, "What It Takes To Be Great," claims that there's only one thing separating great individuals from the rest of us: demanding practice and hard work. They have some interesting ideas that initiate discussion, but we say there's more to greatness than "demanding practice."

Author Geoffrey Colvin, *Fortune* senior editor-at-large, begins by disputing the notion that great people are "preordained" or "destined" to greatness because of some innate quality. He cites a British study by Howe, Davidson, and Sluboda to assert this. We respectfully agree and disagree.

We agree because everyone benefits when the "innate skills" concept is eliminated or minimized. Without that limiting concept, we can believe that each of us can achieve some level of greatness. We also note that just because one was born with a gift does not mean one will use it.

But we also cannot entirely reject the concept of innate gifts. Research and data in "Now, Discover Your Strengths" by Clifton and Buckingham, among other studies, indicate that we have "talents" that enable us to do some things more easily than others. We have natural abilities that if cultivated will allow us to develop more easily if we focus on them.

We do agree with Colvin that nothing happens without hard work. No matter our natural talent, if we don't develop, practice, and hone that gift, we will never achieve greatness. To surpass others we do, it seems, have to "practice, practice, practice." And yet many of us have practiced diligently, only to develop incrementally. We never seem to take the leaps that would land us into the realm of greatness.

Here's where Colvin's article offers something powerful and applicable: Florida State University professor K. Ericsson's studies of individuals who have achieved greatness in their field. What Ericsson discovered is that "deliberate practice" makes perfect. Colvin defines deliberate practice as "activity that's explicitly intended to improve performance, that reaches for objectives just beyond one's level of competence, provides feedback on results, and involves high levels of repetition."

Any pursuit involves repeatable behaviors. By isolating those behaviors that lead to success, getting feedback about how we engage in them, and using that feedback to practice on a daily basis can make it possible for anyone to become great.

So, why don't we do it? Again, we have to agree with Colvin: it's too much hard work. For most of us it's difficult enough to get through the day without adding feedback and repeated practice. This is essentially what separates great individuals from the rest of us; they are motivated to continue practicing. But no one has been able to figure out why some people are driven to deliberate practice. Maybe that's the innate piece Colvin does not believe in.

Either way, there is some comfort and some challenge. None of us can relax behind the notion that since we weren't born with some great gift we can never become great. We can. The comfort is the fact that with deliberate practice any of us can achieve greatness. The challenge is to practice deliberate practice day after day.

Are You a "Greatness Project?"

December 2006

While reviewing four years of articles, we've noticed how we've focused primarily on presenting current research about great individual or organizational successes. As this year ends, we return to our root inquiry about greatness and ask: what about us? How do we foster our own personal growth and development?

At ASGMC we encounter many, many people who are trying to succeed. They tell us about all the projects they're working on in their professional lives and perhaps even at home. Mostly these projects are things to accomplish. Occasionally, we'll meet someone who balances outside projects with "inner" projects. They work toward becoming a better person, parent, lover, boss, etc., focusing not on what they do, but on who they are.

While reading this we hope many of you immediately think, "I do that!" Our question is this: do you develop for yourself the same kind of process, time frame, and sequence that you'd use in a work or home project?

For many of us, ideas for developing ourselves are haphazard at best. At New Year's we create resolutions — that we keep for a while. Usually they fade out in a month or so, only to be replaced by spasms of guilt when we realize how far we've fallen from our personal goal.

We suggest creating a plan of action for personal growth and development similar to project plans we create elsewhere. This would include starting with a specific and well articulated goal. What do you want to be, learn, or become better at? What, for example, would it mean to become a better friend? It might mean

149

better communication, since it's easy to lose touch with friends. The specificity of this goal will help you attain it. You can make the goal be even more specific by enumerating the times a month you'll try contacting someone. You might say, "This is artificial." We agree, but all practice feels artificial until it becomes part of us.

Next, create a timeline. When can you accomplish your stated goal? If it's a lifelong goal, at which points along the way will you check to see if you're on target? Establishing a timeline will help you hold yourself accountable; don't wish your life away on "someday."

Finally, don't forget to use the proper tools. Depending on your focus, your tools could be anything from books, to classes, to friends and counselors, to spirituality or faith (embodied in participating at a house of worship or not), to practice and development with a teacher or mentor.

Many of us are good at finishing whatever work is presented to us, but what about the work you want to do on yourself? Greatness is not only about doing great things for others, it's also about doing great things to enhance your best self.

Have you made yourself a "greatness project?"

Pressure Is a Privilege

January 2007

> *"Instead of thinking how great I've got it, I think about how much more work I have ahead of me and how much more practicing I need to do to become better at what I do."*
> — *Kenny G, Grammy award winning saxophonist*

As we evolve our Greatness Project through on-going research and coaching individuals around the world, we continue to learn that the work of great individuals is never complete. Skilled individuals, like a Kenny G and others strive constantly to do what they do even better. Driven by success rather than by fear of failure, they willingly create new enterprises in quest of the one thing that will make a difference in their life and the lives of others.

Think Brad Pitt (Make It Right Foundation), Nicholas Negroponte (One Laptop Per Child), Jack Sim (World Toilet Organization), Wendy Kopp (Teach for America), or Zainab Salbi (Women for Women) to mention only a very few trying to change the world for the better. I'm sure you can think of many other social entrepreneurs who use their talents to make the world a better place. Are you one of them?

It takes a good deal of courage and curiosity to achieve greatness for yourself and others. We're rarely ever surprised anymore when seemingly average performers become defensive when we suggest new ways for them to become better. They'll often say that they don't really need to learn anything new because they have it "all figured out" or they are "good enough." And yet, I often think of a text message from Billy Jean King to Maria Sharapova before her finals match at the 2008 Australian Open, "Champions take chances and pressure is a privilege."

What chances are you taking to achieve greatness? Do you enjoy pressure or do you try to avoid it? In their new book *The Power of Unreasonable People: How Social Entrepreneurs Create Markets That Change the World* by John Elkington et al., the authors suggest that individuals who are achieving great things for themselves or others are never satisfied. Once a project is up and running they look for the next idea. Are you satisfied with your place in the universe, or are you a champion that loves the pressure of trying to achieve in different and perhaps better ways? Are you challenging yourself to become even better than you thought possible? How much pressure are you willing to withstand to create more justice in the world? Finally we ask, "What one small change might you undertake to have the greatest impact on you and the world?"

Greatness and Newton's Law of Inertia

February 2007

"A body at rest tends to stay at rest while a body in motion tends to stay in motion traveling at a constant speed and in a straight line until acted upon by an outside force."
— *Sir Isaac Newton: The Law of Inertia*

Is there an easy way to achieve greatness? This seems to be an unspoken underlying question whenever we work with groups or individuals. People want a magic key that will unlock their full potential and of course they want it quickly and easily. Meanwhile, they delay pursuit of their own greatness, becoming a body at rest. They'll admit, "I've always wanted to…" or "I've got this great idea, but I've never…" while their potential remains largely untested.

What keeps you at rest? What delays you from pursuing your own greatness project? Most self-help books identify either the fear of success or the fear of failure. Our empirical evidence suggests another reason for remaining at rest: the success of the endeavor we've chosen is so grand that we're intimidated before we begin. When we think about all the hours and calculate all the work, we become exhausted. It's easier to stay at rest and chat about how much we'd like to pursue our greatness.

The first step toward greatness involves identifying what keeps you at rest. Are your reasons — and you'll probably have more than one — internal or external? Internal reasons include: fear of success or failure; being overwhelmed by the task; identity issues (i.e., "What will people think of me if I do this?"); or simply lack of drive or desire. External reasons are generally driven by survival (e.g., "I need this job to survive."); family responsibilities; financial well-being (e.g., "I can't afford to leave this," or "I can't afford to start something new.") or physical challenges. Your resting might be a combination of both internal and external reasons. We invite you to identify your reason(s) for staying at rest. Doing this is essential before taking the next step.

After identifying your reason for resting, select the best "force" to apply. What will shove you off your resting place and move you toward greatness? Each of us will answer this in a particular, personal way. A friend regaled us with his story and what moved him. For years he had been thinking about starting his own business but was very comfortable where he was. He had a good job with a reputable firm, was moving up the corporate ladder, and seemed very secure. What he hated was the politics and he wanted to get out, but could not muster the courage. One day, he was summoned by human resources and told that his entire group was about to be disbanded. He would be out of a job. However, since he was such a good employee, they had three job offers for him. He replied that he would let them know his decision later. When he realized the company, if they let him go, would offer him a package that he could use to start his business, he took the plunge. He has now been in his own business for a full year and is very successful, but admits he needed the push to get out.

The push we just described is a bit dramatic. We don't wish that on anyone. However, we do have to identify the push or pull that will move us forward. If you haven't moved forward because you fear either failure or success, the push might involve examining your life and examining successes you've already achieved. This reality check will help you see that you're a person who succeeds and you can do so again. If your reason is external, you might want to take small steps toward greatness without putting yourself or loved ones at risk.

Far too often we hear the "woulda, coulda, shoulda" talk whenever we bring up greatness. We all have dreams and desires, so why does it seem that only a special few achieve them? What holds you back from at least starting? What is keeping you at rest? Remember: a body in motion stays in motion. It's much easier to keep going once you've gotten started. So, start already! Become great.

Hearing Voices?
March 2007

Three weeks ago, we spoke at a conference for financial service professionals. Beginning the session we asked, "How many of you hear voices?" There was general laughter and a few comments like, "Only when I go off the deep end." After admitting we were kidding, we clarified our question by asking, "How many of you, when you are attempting something new, never tried, or something outside of your comfort zone, say to yourself, 'I can't do this' or 'I've never tried something like this' or 'What if it fails?'" We asked for a show of hands. Eventually, almost every hand in the room was raised, although all attending were successful professionals. Whether we're starting a personal greatness project or attempting something new at work or home, it seems the "limiting voices" are sometimes louder than the "encouraging voices."

What is a limiting voice? It's the internal voice warning us about possible danger. Essential for survival, it alerts us to the potential threats of any new undertaking so we can remain safe or at least be prepared. Unfortunately, this limiting voice does not stay silent when there's a possibility for innovation or change because these shatter the status quo and may place us at risk. There's a place for a limiting voice when we attempt new things. Otherwise, we might become too vulnerable and fail to protect ourselves from possible failure.

When, however, a limiting voice becomes our dominant reaction to change and innovation, any possibility of growth is stifled. No longer protecting us from danger, an unfettered limiting voice may prevent us from exploring any new ideas, relationships, or business possibilities.

Limiting voices take many forms. Some keep us in check by constantly reminding us where we fall short: "I can't do this." "I'm out of my league here." "I'm a loser." Some of us listen to limiting voices that focus on external factors: "They are out to get me." "These things always turn out badly." "That is just too hard to do."

Most self-help books emphasize focusing only on the positive. However, we find that individuals who rise to greatness have a keen awareness of inherent dangers. When internal warnings sound, they listen. What's different is in their reaction. Great individuals do not fight limiting voices by ignoring them or throwing positive platitudes at them; they gauge the seriousness of the warning and reframe what they hear into an encouraging voice.

An encouraging voice is the one that, in response to a perceived threat, seeks options, demands positive movement, and is based on reality. Great individuals examine previous successes and compare them to the uncertainty (i.e., threat) of whatever they're about to undertake. Next, they consider either a question: "Am I really out of my league here?" Or, they assert: "New undertakings have mostly turned out well for me." Listening to this encouraging voice will allow us to become energized rather than defeated.

Many of us are challenged by the volume and constancy of the limiting voices each time we desire to attempt something new, or develop ourselves. Limiting voices can be useful to help us gauge the danger of whatever we're attempting. But it's only by transforming them into encouraging voices that we can move forward with energy toward our goal.

Don't Wait to Act!
April 2007

When asked their age, children tend to round up to the nearest year or half year. "I'm almost four," they'll say with pride. Young children dream of being big kids and play act as such. We wonder why they rush to grow up, yet contained in their play acting there's a valid learning style. This learning style is also present in great individuals and we can adopt it.

Young children learn mostly through observation and mimicry. They play school, house, etc., based on what they've seen and heard. Experiential play is how they learn to be an adult, a mommy or daddy, a professional. Occasionally this method of learning helps them change their mind when they realize, through play acting, that they don't want that particular career. Whatever their decision, they learn by acting "as if" they are already in that particular job or are that particular person.

Many books tout the importance of being in the moment. This great advice allows us to focus on what is right in front of us. Being able to live and think as if a future goal is already reality is also a great skill to have. We've noticed that great individuals have this ability. They act as if they've already attained the goal they seek. We note that forethought is defined in the **American Heritage College Dictionary** as "deliberation, consideration, or planning beforehand. Preparation or thought for the future." We'd like to differentiate this characteristic of acting as if a future goal has already been achieved by naming it "foreaction."

Foreaction serves to jump-start the achievement of any goal or greatness project. Once we've established the goal (e.g., owning our own business), we begin acting as if we already own our own business. Foreacting swiftly affects the way we perceive the world. We're more open to opportunities and pitfalls. In our example, we would think as a business owner rather than a person hoping to be a business owner. Foreacting helps clarify what we look at and how we decide our next steps.

We grow more confident as we foreact because living out our dream, goal or greatness project allows us to experience goal completion. We carry ourselves differently because we're living in the reality of our achieved goal. Rather than approaching the goal tentatively, we convey confidence.

Finally, foreaction creates a self-fulfilling prophecy. When we already believe we've achieved our goal, we tend to identify and take the necessary steps for success instead of just thinking about them. This acting-believing-living process propels our hesitation into action, our hope into belief and our distant goal into our current reality.

A learning pattern that allows children to develop at an amazing rate is also present in great individuals who do not wait until a goal is reached to live and act differently. Foreaction is a skill we can cultivate to propel us toward our goals and help us achieve them more quickly.

Turn Up the Volume
May 2007

Children's exuberance is often hushed with the admonition, "use your inside voice." Well- trained children immediately modulate their volume so they're more acceptable according to their parents' societal norms. Even on a playground they'll be shushed so they're not overly obnoxious to others playing nearby or, perhaps, to their auditory-overloaded parent. While this may be considered a way to teach good manners, this mild form of repression has deeper repercussions as we grow older, ones that don't quite support a movement toward greatness.

Well intentioned as it may be, inhibiting exuberance, emotions, ideas, passions, or spontaneity gradually creates an internal predisposition to blending in. The so-called mature person is quiet, reflective, soft-spoken and wise; that's fine, if that's their authentic disposition. For many, the demand to fit dampens energy, enthusiasm and determination to be or do something different. The philosopher Henry David Thoreau wrote, "Most men [and women] lead lives of *quiet* desperation and go to the grave with the song still in them" (emphasis ours). However, great individuals are not characterized by Thoreau's description.

What is the alternative? Novelist, Emile Zola answers, "If you ask me what I came into this life to do, I will tell you: I came to live *out loud*" (emphasis ours). By promoting Zola, we're not suggesting a change in parenting rules; we live in a communal society where civility is necessary. We need to develop ways for children and adults to learn how to modulate their tone without modulating their lives. Great individuals live life fully and powerfully. They're not inhibited by internal constraint to modulate the power of their ideas, or their impact on society. They give free reign to their internal and external voice to deliver powerful, passionate, promising ideas that scream to be heard.

The initial societal reaction to someone living out loud is to tell them to quiet down. We don't seem to like those who stand out from the rest of us. This reaction was once necessary for survival. In early civilization, an individual standing out or being too loud could endanger the entire tribe. We no longer need to curb our initial exuberance because the survival imperative doesn't apply for most of us.

We'd be more honest if we'd simply admit that we feel awkward when someone dares to show their greatness by living out loud. And when we applaud their accomplishments, isn't there an introspective moment when we realize that we are also capable of such greatness? When that happens, do we accept that challenge or do we create reasons why we cannot achieve greatness?

What does living out loud really mean? Initially, it means setting ourselves free from our own internal censor. We need to silence the voices that warn us not to stand out, not to think differently, not to be noticed. Instead, we need to turn up the volume on our original thoughts, enthusiasm, joy, and passion. This freedom of thought allows for the greatest creativity and expression.

Eventually the volume inside will become audible. It's not that we'll have unregulated outbursts, but as we feel increasingly free to express what we're thinking and feeling, we'll set ourselves aside from grim-faced work warriors. A life, given free reign, demands to be noticed, not ignored and is manifested through enthusiasm, passion, joy and excitement in everything the person does.

Turning up the volume of our lives will also create some challenges for others. As we noted earlier, people tend to distance themselves from and even dislike those who stand out. Essential to our growth and development will be a support network of like-minded individuals who encourage us.

Our lives come with a mute button; internal controls that hold us back from standing out. Fortunately we choose how those controls are used. As we move toward realizing our greatness, we must allow the power and volume of our lives free reign. When that happens, there will be no stopping us.

Be Startled!

June-July 2007

Ray Bradbury, in the Afterword of his novel, *Farewell Summer* (2006) acknowledged, "Surprise is everything with me. When I go to bed at night I give instructions to startle myself when I wake in the morning. That was one of the great adventures in letting this novel evolve: my instructions at night and being startled in the morning by revelations." In a similar manner, individuals striving for greatness are willing to be startled.

Seven years after beginning our inquiry into greatness, characteristics and attributes still continue to come forth clamoring to be noticed. We've noticed the consistent presence of an attitude that seems present in individuals striving toward greatness and missing in others: a willingness to learn; to "be startled" by new awareness and insights. We first became aware of this while monitoring the response to new ideas among those we've coached, counseled, and taught. Most often, individuals at or near the top of their field were open to new concepts, willing to hear new ideas, and willing to be challenged. We found the opposite to be true among those who, although good in their respective professions, were not generally acknowledged as great. These individuals were often defensive and obstinate; believing they already knew what there was to know. They approached every learning opportunity certain that they had the answer. There's no startling them.

Individuals striving for greatness, however, conveyed their willingness to learn through: 1) an internal predisposition; 2) a malleable sense of self; and 3) inquisitiveness about new thoughts and ideas.

Regarding internal predisposition, we found that individuals striving for greatness approach life with a willingness and desire to learn. Although driven and focused, they're nevertheless open to new possibilities and information. Many of us grew up accustomed to parents asking, "What did you learn today?" and expecting an answer. Now that no one asks, it's up to us to approach life with a predisposition to learning. At ASGMC, we're committed to being curious, not certain. Following this principle means we put aside our certainty for the moment and become open to the possibility of what is new. Establishing this internal disposition helps us "see" learning opportunities. Otherwise, we're blinded by our own self-aggrandizement to what others or new opportunities offer.

Along with an internal predisposition toward learning comes an increased openness to learning about self. To know oneself has always been viewed as the foundation of growth and development. If we believe we are complete, that there's no more inner work to be done, we miss opportunities for development. Every interaction, every moment contains information that illumines the self. How we react, respond, and move forward provides valuable information about how others see us, how we see ourselves, and the possible disparity between these viewpoints. Our willingness to explore interactions with others strengthens our emotional IQ and also enhances our ego strength.

Finally our experience reveals that great individuals seek new ideas. They welcome new ways of doing things, thinking, or developing. They arm themselves with an attitude of, "I'll learn or take away one new thing." Because they approach learning encounters this way, they're assured of discovering additional information or ways of doing something, even if it's finding out what won't work.

Great individuals willingly engage in dialogue, read works outside their comfort zone, and try to evaluate all information objectively to glean the most information out of it.

Want to enter the realm of greatness? Commit to an internal predisposition toward learning; become willing to hear new things about yourself and respond accordingly; try out new ideas and actions. Be startled by what you experience and become great.

Are You Flourishing?
August 2007

Think about your typical day. Are you functioning at a high level? Are you happy and satisfied with what you're doing? Do you enjoy creativity? Are you willing to be flexible in various areas of your life? When you experience difficulties, do you bounce back quickly? If you answer "yes" to most of these questions, then you are flourishing. If you have some doubt, or wish to flourish more in your life and your work, read on.

Flourishing is defined as living "within an optimal range of human functioning, one that connotes goodness, generativity, growth and resilience." This simple definition is the springboard for an article by Barbara Fredrickson and Marcial Losada, "Positive Affect and The Complex Dynamics of Human Flourishing" (**American Psychologist**, Oct. 2005). Their work on flourishing can impact the way we speak to each other, who we connect with and perhaps even our self talk.

Fredrickson and Losada contrast flourishing with languishing which they understand as "people who describe their lives as 'hollow' or 'empty.'" Citing research indicating that only 20% of U.S. adults flourish, they advocate embracing the mental, physical, and organizational benefits of flourishing. They focused their research on how positive affect leads to flourishing. In practical, empirical terms this means receiving enough positive comments, interactions, and successes to overcome the negative affect we experience each day.

Whenever we've asked individuals how many positive comments or responses they receive in a day, they usually answer "zero." And yet, while receiving little or no positive affect they're expected to perform at tremendously high levels. Even without reading the research, we know maintaining high performance without affirmation is very difficult to do. Marriages experience the same challenges and predictability. When researchers coded the positive and negative comments couples made to each other, there was a direct relation between how many positive comments the couples shared per day and marital longevity. So, if there's evidence that positive affect leads to flourishing, can we employ positive affect to flourish in our lives?

The answer is yes and no. We cannot create flourishing if the positive affect is faked. As humans, we can see right through insincere positive affect. What does work in our favor is the fact that the various components of positive affect—positive thinking, acting and feeling—can stimulate one another. Positive thinking can trigger positive acting and/or feeling and visa versa. This reality alone allows us to create dynamics where the more positive affect can be experienced the more negative affect can be overcome. For example, if in your work you deliberately offer positive affect by praising good work and focusing on the good things going on during the day, you can create an environment in which everyone can flourish, leading to short and long term success.

But real life dictates that occasionally we may have to say something negative to someone else. How we express that negativity can have a great deal to do with the impact it will have. If the negativity is time-limited, with realistic feedback focused on a specific situation, it will not substantially affect the individual adversely. However, when the negative affect is constant, unfocused and universal (e.g., "you always do the wrong thing") then it will hamper individuals from flourishing.

What kind of day would you prefer? One that involves flourishing or languishing? Each of us has the opportunity to foster flourishing by creating opportunities to experience positive affect throughout our day. We can do this by the way we speak to each other, our choices of associates, and how we think about our work and ourselves. As Fredrickson and Losada summarize, "Human flourishing is optimal functioning…" Isn't that what we want every day?

From High to Low and Back Again
September 2007

By Charles Wasilewski

2006 was a fantastic year for me as a sports fan. My Rutgers football team went undefeated through nine games and cruised to its first-ever bowl game victory. I was sky-high. My family and I enjoyed a great trip to Houston for that Texas Bowl game, which the Scarlet Knights won handily, 37-10 over Big 12 team Kansas State.

Back home after that memorable and inspiring trip, I wanted to extend my excitement and do something new to support my favorite team. While I had donated money over the years and attended games both dreary and delightful, I saw new opportunities.

Around that time I read ASGMC's THE GREATNESS PROJECT challenging me to come up with a new goal. So I dreamed up the idea of a Web site to emphasize the "Just Keep Chopping" rallying cry that Rutgers football leans on. ("Just Keep Chopping" is the slogan that head coach Greg Schiano came up with, based on a story about being lost in the thick woods: You just have to pick up your ax and start chopping; pretty soon, if you keep chopping you'll be able to find your way out.) I thought I'd come up with a logo and merchandise that would capture this idea and I'd share the proceeds with Rutgers.

Now I'm naïve, but not naïve enough to think that the little effort I was starting would amount to much of a difference in a place with a multi-billion dollar budget such as a university. Still, I wanted to tap into my passion for the sport and the university and give back a little something to a team that had inspired me during some tough times.

Then the obstacles started popping up. There were the usual challenges: coming up with ideas, researching merchandise, setting a budget, finding the right resources, and promoting the idea. I also discovered that the university had filed for copyright registration for the term "Keep Chopping." That was fine, but it meant that I had to get approval from a bureaucracy for anything I did. Without going into specifics, let me just say that that process proved to be trying before it was fruitful.

The roadblock was significant enough that I asked myself: "Why am I bothering to do this?" After all, this was a hobby, not a job, something to enjoy in my spare time to feed my passion. The answer surprised me.

I found out I was not doing it for Rutgers, or for the team, or for the fans. Yes, all those people and things inspired me, but I found out I was doing this because I wanted to. I wanted to support an idea - and found out I still do, even with the roadblocks and obstacles.

The $160 donation I made as a share of the proceeds from t-shirts and books sold through ChopChamps.com might not sound like much. But, in retrospect, I'd pay a whole lot more to learn what I did: don't do something because you expect something back; do it because you love to.

Charles Wasilewski is a businessperson and Rutgers graduate who started fan web site ChopChamps.com in 2007. He can be reached at info@Chopchamps.com.

Wanting What You Want to Want

October 2007

Recently we rediscovered two major obstacles in the progression toward individual greatness. One is focusing our willpower on what we want to accomplish. Let's face it, many of us are easily distracted from goals and dreams. But we face a larger impediment before we can focus our willpower. We don't know what we want. We became aware of this while participating in an experiment by Dr. James Pawelski at the University of Pennsylvania.

Pawelski offers an exercise intended to increase the attention on wanting what we want to want. Briefly, "Wanting What You Want To Want" (WWYWW) involves helping someone focus on the reasons they want something and strengthening their will (William James defined will as the effort of attention). Once the will is strengthened the individual becomes self-motivated.

As we tried the experiment, it became apparent that the first challenge involved knowing what we really want. Over the years, we've discovered that many people have long ago put aside their dreams, wishes, goals and aspirations and have difficulty reconstructing them. When we've asked people to identify what they wanted to want, they had difficulty doing this because so many other "wants" have gotten in the way. We've identified some of these superimposed "wants."

Wanting What Society Wants Me to Want (WWSWMW). Society generates certain expectations. Some of them are necessary for society to function (i.e., laws, customs, language). Some expectations have been imposed by tradition, history and common practice (i.e., expectations of men vs. women, acting as an "adult", etc.).

Wanting What the Media Wants Me to Want (WWMWMW). Many of us find ourselves driven by what the media wants us to want. We focus on the new BMW or a bigger house. We stress about holidays because we attempt to replicate Hallmark commercials of the perfect family with their perfect holiday dinner scene.

Wanting What My Parents (family) Want Me to Want (WWPWMW). From an early age, either blatantly or by sharing desires, parents superimpose their desires on us. Despite the process of individuation, we still carry the desires our parents have for us. Some of us, never completing individuation process, are still trying to fulfill our parents' wishes.

These are just a few of the "wants" we found that impeded people from identifying what they want to want. You may be able to identify a few more that impede you. How then can we discover what we really want to want? The process is two-fold, and takes time, quiet and some attention.

First, we need to identify all of the wants that are driven by others. Sorting through those wants we need to determine whether to keep or get rid of them. Second, we need to really listen to our inner desires and dreams—again! Many of us put our wants aside when we entered school, or as we progressed in our lives. We thought we were being selfish by focusing on what we wanted rather than on someone else. It's not selfish to know what you want. It's self-discovery and growth.

Having identified what we want to want, we can now focus on developing the strength of will we need to achieve what we want. Great individuals are very clear about what they want and focus all their will power to achieve it.

When Greatness Gets a Push
November 2007

Sometimes greatness needs a push. Greatness can seemingly lie dormant for many years. All it takes is a moment when something or someone threatens our beliefs and values. But these moments present opportunities for us to rise to new heights, change our lives and reveal our inherent greatness. We've all had these life-changing moments and will continue to have them. How can we make the most of them?

Parameshwar Srikantia in his 2001 doctoral dissertation, *The Architecture of Greatness*, researched greatness by studying thirty eminent philosophers' ideas about greatness and then compared these with the results of his interviews with individuals in South Asia and Africa. He discovered that critical incidents or turning-points that inevitably led to a life of greatness could be identified. Srikantia noted how critical incidents share a configuration of four elements that combine to propel ~~ind~~ividuals to new and extraordinary courses of action.

Srikantia found the first element is an "antecedent condition, a presenting situation that involves a fundamental threat to one's personal equilibrium." This condition jars individuals out of complacency into action. When their values, beliefs or personal goals come under attack they fight back. Based on our findings from THE GREATNESS PROJECT, we would expand this notion of a presenting situation to include positive opportunities as well as threats. These moments may occur in small daily challenges and big life-changing challenges. The critical moment comes when, having acknowledged the threat or opportunity, you decide whether to take up the challenge. At this point greatness moves some of us forward, others stall.

The second element is what Srikantia calls "The Mayflower phenomenon." Just as the people on the Mayflower brought ideas and values to forge a new land, so too do those moving toward greatness bring images of greatness learned from important individuals or experiences. These images form us. Story, song, history, and family all play a part in creating our personal notion of greatness to be unleashed at the necessary moment. Taking time to cultivate your notion of greatness and identify those who have contributed to your ideas and beliefs will serve you well at these critical moments.

Third, Srikantia found that the action taken from the critical incident expands possibilities for others, not only for oneself. The presenting threat or opportunity may reveal something larger at stake. Great actions and individuals touch others' lives, so it's imperative to examine your response to a critical incident. If your actions won't positively affect others, examine your motives.

The final element emerging from a critical incident is a willingness to pay the price; a propensity to be unstoppable in the pursuit of an ideal. Greatness never goes unchallenged. Whether the adversary is time, nature, other people, or ourselves, perseverance is essential. When the time comes, what will you be willing to do to achieve your goal? How much will you persist?

Critical incidents reveal four elements that can generate greatness. We challenge you to identify your life-changing, life-challenging moments and then learn from them about your values and beliefs. Pay attention to the ideas you've learned about greatness; what it is and how to live it. Watch your actions. See how they touch the lives of those around you, but stay true to your values. Finally, in the words of Winston Churchill, "Never, never, never, give up."

Inner Gifts

December 2007

Though we've just passed the shortest day of the year and the days should be lengthening, it still seems cold and bleak (at least it does in New Jersey). Traditionally this time of year, especially in the colder climates, we moved inside, sat around fires and told stories. More importantly, it was a time for introspection and resolution.

This is also the time of year for gift giving in many cultures. You may have given your gifts already, or are looking forward to your gifting. What about giving a gift to yourself? In this spirit we read a wonderful suggestion of inner gift giving in the December 2007 issue of *Ode Magazine*. The author, Jay Walljasper, suggests twelve days of reflection that help us reconnect with and reignite our inner selves. We quote them in their entirety below as suggestions for reflection.

December 25 – Receptivity: What gifts from the universe have you declined to accept or acknowledge?

December 26 – Generosity: Think of three people and what you can give of yourself to them.

December 27 – Humility: Think about how humility can become a great source of strength and power for you.

December 28 – Nobility: Make a list of people from whose noble qualities you can learn.

December 29 – Solidity: For 12 minutes simply feel your life's solidity.

December 30 – Fluidity: Consider the importance of flow to your well-being and happiness.

December 31 – Luminosity: Look back at your darkest

moments of the last year, and remember what qualities in yourself and others lit the way for you.

January 1 – Reflectivity: Let an image from the outer world settle in your mind and write down five thoughts you associate with it. Reflect on it and how you might transform it.

January 2 – Equanimity: Pick a recent event and review it in light of various possible emotions like happiness, anger and fear.

January 3 – Fecundity: Celebrate the richness of your imagination. Hold this vision and then plan tomorrow's activities. Keep it alive during the day.

January 4 – Sagacity: Think of yourself as an elder who has learned from the trials and triumphs of experience. What are some profound lessons?

January 5 – Unity: What ideas, yearnings, themes or insights have come together for you through the holidays?

Reflections Appendix

"If you experience limiting voices when you attempt something new or seek personal growth, experiment with turning them into encouraging voices." The following questions provide a process to help you turn discouragement to positive action.

- List your internally-focused limiting voices. (Examples: "I'm a loser." "I can't do this." "I have to do everything perfectly.")
- Create encouraging voices based on your life's reality. (Examples: "I've succeeded in a lot of things." "I can try to do this." "I can continue to do my best at everything I attempt.")
- List any limiting voices about things external to you. (Examples: "These new ideas always turn out badly." "They are out to get me.")
- Create encouraging voices based on the reality of your life and experience. (Examples: "Some of the new ideas I've had have been well accepted." "This group is wary of change, but they've liked what I've offered before.")

Foreaction involves identifying a goal and then realizing how you would feel, think, and act if the goal were realized. Below are a few questions to help you cultivate this discipline.

- Identify a specific goal you would like to achieve. (For those who are committed to being a Greatness Project use that goal.)
- How would you feel if you achieved this goal? How would those feelings manifest every day?
- How would you act if you had achieved this goal? What would be different in your daily life?
- What would change about how to see yourself in the world if you achieved this goal?
- How can you act/believe/live differently right now to reflect what you hope to achieve?

Consider some of these questions for reflection to assist you in allowing you to live your life out loud.

- When thinking or acting in an innovative or creative way what are the first negative thoughts that curb your creativity, enthusiasm, or expression of the new concept?

- If you find yourself standing out, what goes through your mind that might make you withdraw and retreat?

- Examining your initial "muting" thoughts above, rewrite them below so they are encouraging, and supportive of creativity and expression.

- Create a way to remind yourself to replace your "muting" internal statements with the encouraging internal statements you have created and repeat them in your mind until they become your initial response to your own creativity and uniqueness.

Some questions to consider as you reflect on being startled.

- What is your internal disposition toward learning? Why?

- What have you recently learned about yourself or about how others perceive you? (If you have not recently learned anything, why do you think that might be?)

- Where in your life are you exploring new ideas or new ways of doing things?

Some questions to consider at the end of each day as you reflect on flourishing.

- Where/when was I happy, satisfied, and functioning at a high level today?
- When did I allow myself to think and act differently? When was I flexible?
- What did I do for myself today? How did I endeavor to expand/reinforce my social network today?
- How did I respond to adversity today?

The Greatness Project Challenge

Great individuals are often described as larger than life. Reality dictates, of course, that none of us is larger than life since, eventually, life will continue and we won't. However, this phrase captures something about the essence of great individuals; that somehow their lives are extraordinary. Do you want to be larger than life?

Over the years, we've seen a ten-fold increase in the number of people who receive our monthly essays. Additionally, we know of leaders and managers who, once they receive it, send THE GREATNESS PROJECT on to their divisions, organizations, or work force. What we appreciate even more are the emails, stories, or comments we receive from readers. People are thinking about what we write, but are any of us doing things differently?

Our focus this month is inspired by an article in the January 2007 issue of *National Geographic*. "Arctic Nightmare" follows two extreme explorers as they attempt to travel (ski, walk, and swim) to the North Pole during the Arctic winter. As gripping as the account is, the mindset of these men was what drew us in. Author Marguerite Del Giudice notes that, "It isn't a desire to be closer to death that attracts them, they will tell you. It's a desire to be closer to life. They know that willpower can be built, that ordinary people, like themselves, have abilities beyond their reckonings."

What are your capabilities? Have you really tested your limits? Many of us would say that we're comfortable. We've managed to create lives of peaceful coexistence with the world and we move through our lives gently crossing days off the calendar. What if we began a movement to live great lives? We're not suggesting a walk to the North Pole, but what if we actively choose to be closer to life by challenging ourselves to find — and go beyond — the current limits of our abilities?

We invite you to choose an area for exploration — becoming a great parent, boss, or peer; or attempting something you've always desired to do; or growing to become the best person you could possibly be. We invite you to join us in going further than you've ever allowed yourself to go toward personal greatness.

No, you don't have to sign up, you don't have to join. We simply offer this as a catalyzing challenge. This is not about fame or fortune, but a desire to be closer to life.

The Greatness Project Challenge:
Initial Steps

These questions are presented for you to answer privately. Their intention is to help you take the first steps toward your personal Greatness Project. Take time and think about each of these areas. Especially focus on what might inhibit you from initializing your project; this will help you identify what force you can use to energize yourself and your project.

Project Name or Description: _____

Factors Inhibiting Initiation of Greatness Project:
(choose one or more that apply and describe it for yourself)

- Internal
  - ❑ Fear of success _____
  - ❑ Fear of failure _____
  - ❑ Identity issues _____
  - ❑ Overwhelmed with size of project _____
  - ❑ Other _____

- External
  - ❑ Family issues _____
  - ❑ Financial issues_____
  - ❑ Physical limitations (personal or structural – if a building is involved) _____
  - ❑ Other_____

_____

Identify the force to be applied to whatever is inhibiting you so you create the initial movement toward your Greatness Project: (be as specific as possible)

- Rational listing of past successes _____
- Creating overall plan _____
- Enlisting the assistance of others: mentor, friend, coach _____

  _____

- Identifying small, possible, immediate steps _____

  _____

- Other _____

  _____

What are the steps you can take this week that will produce an immediate result? _____

_____

_____

_____

_____

How will you celebrate your success at the end of the week?

_____

_____

_____

Works Cited

April 2001
On the Essi System, see: www.essisystems.com.

September 2001
On Leadership, Breakthrough Leadership. *Harvard Business Review* (Special Issue, December 2001).

November 2001
"Personal Histories: Leaders Remember the Moments and People That Shaped Them." *Harvard Business Review* (December 2001): 27-38.

December 2001
Koestenbaum, Peter *Leadership: The Inner Side of Greatness*. San Francisco: Jossey-Bass, 1991.

February 2002
Slater, Robert *Jack Welch and the GE Way*. New York: McGraw Hill, 1998.

April 2002
Blanchard, Ken The Heart of a Leader. Tulsa: Honor Books, 1999.

May 2002
Welch, Jack and John A. Byrne *Jack Straight from the Gut*. New York: Warner Books, 2001.

July 2002
"The Need for Space." *USA Today* (Living Section, July 11, 2002):1.
Frankl, Viktor E. *Man's Search for Meaning*. New York: Washington Square Books, 1984.

October 2002
Stockdale, James E. James E. *Stockdale: A Vietnam Experience*. Palo Alto: Hoover Press, 1984.
Bennis, Warren G. and Robert J. Thomas "Crucibles of Leadership." *Harvard Business Review* (September 2002):39-48.

November 2002
Carter, Jimmy *Bottom Line* (November 2002).

December 2002
Friedman, Stewart *Knowledge@Wharton* (November 20, 2002).

January 2003
Maslow, Abraham *The Further Reaches of Human Nature*. New York: Viking Press, 1971.

May 2003

Lao-Tzu, *Tao Te Ching*. Indianapolis: Hacket Publishing Co., 1993.

June 2003

Wiseman, Richard *The Luck Factor: Changing Your Luck, Changing Your Life, Four Essential Principles*. New York: Hyperion Press, 2003.

July 2003

Bronson, Po *What Should I Do with My Life?* New York: Random House, 2002.

September 2003

"The Fifty Most Powerful Women." *Fortune* (September 2003).

October 2003

May, Rollo *The Courage to Create*. New York: W.W. Norton and Co., 1975.
Fox, Matthew *Creativity*. New York: Putnam Books, 2002.

November 2003

Gelb, Michael *How to Think Like Leonardo da Vinci*. New York: Delacorte Press, 1998.

December 2003

Dalai Lama, *The Art of Happiness*. New York: Penguin Books, 1998.

January 2004

Asalone, Scott and Jan Sparrow, *Invent the Future on Internet* (Radio show aired December, 12, 2003).
Kabat-Zinn, Jon *Wherever You Go; There You Are*. New York: Hyperion, 1995.

March 2004

Nash, Laura and Howard Stevenson, "Success That Lasts." *Harvard Business Review* (February 2004): 102.

June 2004

Lyubomirsky, Sonja "Why Are Some People Happier than Others? The Role of Cognitive and Motivational Processes in Well-being." *American Psychologist* (56): 239-249.

July 2004

See: Freeman, Walter "What's Behind the 4-Minute Mile, Starbucks and the Moon Landing." *Knowledge@Wharton.upenn.edu* June, 2004.
Wind, Yoram and Colin Crook, *The Power of Impossible Thinking*. Upper Saddle River: Wharton School Publishing, 2004.

August 2004

Connellan, Thomas *Bringing Out the Best in Others*. Austin: Bard Press, 2003.

November 2004

Buckingham, Marcus and Donald O. Clifton, *Now, Discover Your Strengths*.
New York: The Free Press, 2001.
Kouzes, James and Barry Posner, *Encouraging the Heart*. San Francisco:
Jossey-Bass, 2003.
Rath, Tom and Donald O. Clifton, *How Full is Your Bucket: Positive Strategies
for Work and Life*. New York: Gallup Press, 2004.

December 2004

Dickens, Charles *A Christmas Carol*. London: Puffin Books, first published in
1843.

January 2005

de Montaigne, Michel trans. by John Cohen., *Montaigne: Essays*. London:
Penguin Books, 1993.

March 2005

Whybrow, Peter *American Mania; When More is Not Enough*. New York: W.W.
Norton and Company, 2005.
Buckingham, Marcus "What Great Managers Do." *Harvard Business Review*
(March 2005):70-79.

April 2005

Murray, Charles *Human Accomplishment*. New York: Harper Collins, 2003.
Rand, Ayn *Atlas Shrugged*. New York: Penguin Books, 1957.

June 2005

Davenport, Thomas and John Beck, *The Attention Economy*. Boston: Harvard
Business School Press, 2001.

July 2005

Hassin, Ran, James Uleman, John Bargh *The New Unconscious*. New York:
Oxford Press, 2005.

October 2005

Bennis, Warren and Robert Thomas *Geeks and Geezers*. Boston: Harvard
Business School Press, 2002.

December 2005

Doskoch, Peter "The Winning Edge." *Psychology Today*
(November/December 2005).

February 2006

Murray, Charles *Human Accomplishment*. New York: Harper Collins, 2003.

April 2006

Murray, Charles *Human Accomplishment*. New York: Harper Collins, 2003.

May 2006

Porras, Jerry, Stewart Emery, and Mark Thompson *Success Built to Last: Creating a Life that Matters*. Upper Saddle River: Wharton Press, 2006.

July 2006

Derber, Charles *The Pursuit of Attention*. Oxford: Oxford Press, 2000.

September 2006

Friend, David *Watching the World Change*. New York: Farrar, Straus and Giroux, 2006.

Luxemburg Income Survey: www.lisproject.org/keyfigures/povertytable.htm

October 2006

Derber, Charles *The Pursuit of Attention*. Oxford: Oxford Press, 2000.

November 2006

Buckingham, Marcus and Donald O. Clifton *Now, Discover Your Strengths*. New York: The Free Press, 2001.

January 2007

Elkington, John *The Power of Unreasonable People: How Social Entrepreneurs Create Markets That Change the World*. Boston: Harvard Press, 2008.

June/July 2007

Bradbury, Ray *Farewell Summer*. New York: HarperCollins, 2006.

August 2007

Fredrickson, Barbara and Losada, Marcial "Positive Affect and the Complex Dynamics of Human Flourishing" *American Psychologist*, October, 2005.

November 2007

Srikantia, Parameshwar "The Architecture of Greatness" *Dissertation Abstracts International*, Section A: Humanities and Social Sciences, 62(1-A)

December 2007

Walljasper, Jay *Ode Magazine*, December, 2007.

SCOTT ASALONE and JAN SPARROW have always been fascinated by human potential. Their initial careers in teaching and ministry allowed them to encourage others through education and self-reflection.

Scott and Jan's paths merged at Merrill Lynch, where they were Vice Presidents in the Leadership and Development Division. In the corporate realm, they analyzed methods and characteristics of the best employees, creating frameworks for others to succeed.

Through A & S Global Management Consulting, which they co-founded in 1999, Jan and Scott have worked with industry leaders, academics, and others to ascertain what distinguishes great individuals, what can be learned from them, and what can be applied to all of our lives.

Scott and Jan regularly present keynotes nationally and internationally, create workshops for organizations, and pursue the study of greatness. Beyond being co-founders of ASGMC, Inc., they are good friends and even neighbors in Trenton, New Jersey.